LET IT BOIL OVER TWICE

LET IT BOIL OVER TWICE

GEORGE CROCKER

A Father And Son Story

GIO Press Ltd

Contents

Copyright		1
Introduction		2
The Author		4
Dedications		5
Acknowledgements		6
1	The Unexpected	7
2	Reminiscing	10
3	Walking Trail	13
4	Hawks Pond	16
5	Red Harbour Falls	23
6	Dreams And Hopes	26
7	Too Soon	31
8	The Uncles	33
9	Hockey Creats Memories	37
10	Christmas	40
11	Traditions	46
12	Carving	52

13	Birthday	58
14	Sibling Secrets	63
15	Schools Out	65
16	Jack	68
17	The Long Walk	75
18	Moose	79
19	The Falls	83
20	The Boil Up	90
21	Peaceful Joy	98
22	Finally	102
23	Gratitude	108
24	Nature's Jacuzzi	115
25	Going Home	118
Authors Update		123

Copyright

Copyright

Let It Boil over Twice 2022 by George Byron Crocker

No part of this publication may be reproduced, distributed, or transmitted in any form or by any means, including photocopy, recording or other electronic or mechanical methods, without the prior written permission of the author, except in case of brief quotation embodied in critical reviews and certain other non-commercial uses permitted by copyright law.

Gio Press Ltd

Email; georgecrocker47@gmail.com

ISBN

978-1-7779158-2-7 (Paperback)

978-1-7779158-3-4 (eBook)

Introduction

This book is based on a father and son relationship. A father who loved his son. The son, Arthur's biggest dream and wish was to go fishing with his dad. As a parent I knew my son really just needed my time more than any other thing he could receive.

My father took me fishing when I was a young boy. One of my most loved and cherished memories of him through the years. My own father passed away some fifty one years ago. I still think about those fishing trips to Hawks pond with such love and thankfulness to have such a father that he was. All sons should be as lucky as me. My father Archibald Crocker gave me, his son, the time both of us needed to make great memories that have lasted beyond his lifetime.

I completed writing this book in April of 2022, fifty One years after the death of my own father. I am thankful to God who listened to my prayers often, I have been able to stay motivated enough to complete it

My son and I have fishing memories that have lasted my lifetime and will live on with him through the years of his life. Our father son story is written inside the pages of this book. I think you will enjoy our story as much as we have enjoyed living it.

When Arthur was a young boy he lived in a salt box style two story house on Mortier Bay, overlooking the ocean. They were a happy family of four. Although his parents had Arthur involved in baseball and hockey he never excelled in sports, but enjoyed playing just for fun. He dreamed of fishing with his dad.

During the difficult time Arthur's father was in early recovery from a TBI, they reminisced about his dream to go fishing at Red Harbour Falls Ponds with his dad. This is that story.

The winter months were cold, and perfect for storytelling by the fire. Arthur listened to so many fishing stories about Red Harbour Falls Ponds, as told by his father, his uncles, and their friends. The place became mystical in his mind.

He prayed that his dream would come true. Visiting and fishing at the Red Harbour Falls Ponds with his dad. Finally, one day it happened. Would it be all it could be? Hear that story and experience what a father and son relationship can be when nurtured at a sons young age. This book is based on that true story. The names have been changed.

The author, George Byron Crocker is a native son of Newfoundland Canada, born in the small town of Creston South, Marystown, on Newfoundland's South Coast.

The Author

George, started his working career as a steel worker in the shipyards of Halifax, Nova Scotia and then later the shipyards of Marystown, Newfoundland before returning to college to complete welding Engineering. For twenty years George operated a small business in Halifax, Nova Scotia, Canada.

A community volunteer George served as a member of The Kinsmen club of Marystown Newfoundland, a men's fellowship service club whose prime purpose was to raise money to help kids and to improve sports and medical facilities in the community

Brain injury survivor George volunteered to give back. He has served for six years on the provincial board of Brain Injury Nova Scotia. The Brain Injury Association of Nova Scotia, (BIANS). BIANS was formed to advocate for those recovering from a brain injury in the province of Nova Scotia Canada.

George, began to write his first book 'Threading the Needles of Life" shortly after his release from hospital after a massive stroke. It published in 2017. He soon had an ideal for a second book. This book, "Let It Boil over Twice," is that story, enjoy the journey.

Dedications

This book is dedicated to my father Archibald Richard Crocker
"We live in the voices of our children

Archibald Richard Crocker February 11, 1912 to August 3rd, 1970

Acknowledgements

My appreciation and thanks to my support team, Nancy Irwin, Stefan Crocker, Suzanne Crocker and Charlotte Crocker, for your love and motivation that has kept me going during my writings, The motivation especially during the many times my brain was seemingly unable or unwilling to continue. A special thank you to my girl Nancy for her advice along the journey.

I also recognize the contribution of my good friends Robert (Bob)Swan, John Alphonse (Johnny A.) and Derrick Le Lacheur for the coffee chats and encouragement along the way. Thank You

A special thank you to my family who lived this story with me.

1

The Unexpected

Arthur's phone started ringing while he was at work on his construction job. He was three floors up on scaffolding this morning and had no time to answer it. The phone kept ringing. He thought, maybe there was something wrong, so he descended to check. He noticed there were a few messages from his father's girlfriend Louise. "Your father collapsed on the floor this morning. I am with him now in an ambulance on the way to the hospital. Please get here as soon as you can."

Arthur sprang into action. He contacted his sister Madison, and both agreed to meet at the hospital as soon as they could. A very upset Louise met them at the Hospital Emergency area doors. Their dad was with a team of doctors. Louise was waiting to hear the prognosis. The testing seemed to go on for hours. They knew it was a massive stroke but the tests would show how it had to be dealt with. The doctors advised brain surgery or Bryon would have no quality of life. Bryon and the children's mother had divorced years ago. It was up to Louise and his children now to agree to the surgery. Arthur was now waiting outside the operating room (O.R.), in hope for his father to regain consciousness. The doctors could not guarantee what the short or long term effects of the stroke or surgery would be. There was a chance that the surgery could cause death, but the alternative was bleak, not a way Bryon would want to live. As the family waited outside the O.R. door, nurses came out regularly with updates. Arthur, Louise and Madison paced the floor with worry, waiting for Byron to come out of surgery and hopefully a full recovery.

Finally, hours later, Byron was wheeled out into a recovery room and then later onto the seventh floor of the hospital where the family could join him. This room would be Byron's home for a few weeks. His children and his girlfriend Louise, soon to be fiancé would spend many hours here in this room, by his side, before Byron would be transferred from the hospital for another 90 days of rehabilitation and recovery. at the Nava Scotia Habitation facility

During his rehabilitation stay of ninety days Louise and his children visited every day. During his time in the rehabilitation hospital his family worked with him and hospital staff to make him feel comfortable and positive. They also helped with his rehabilitation, working with speech and occupational therapists (OT), Physiotherapy (PT), social workers, medical doctors and other specialists, planning for his recovery. Although Byron would physically recover, his brain would most likely never be the same.

Over the next months and years, Byron, and his family would gradually come to terms with Byron's new normal. Here now, on the seventh floor, his children watched as Byron lay motionless in his hospital bed with nurses regularly checking on him. His breathing was shallow at times but at least he had kept breathing through the night. It was mid-morning, a lifetime ago it seemed, since they had received the call from Louise.

Later that night, sitting alone by his father's bed watching his father sleep, Arthur's emotions could not be contained and he broke into tears that flowed down his cheeks. He remembered the good times he had enjoyed with his father as a boy. He thought about his father teaching him and Madison to ride their bikes, laughing as he ran behind them, cheering them on.

Arthur remembered watching the Toronto Maple Leaf's hockey games on television with his dad and The Toronto Blue Jay baseball team winning the World Series. He thought about playing catch and how his dad had taught him to catch a baseball. The thoughts raced into Arthur's head in a flurry.

Arthur's thoughts were racing as he relived his beautiful memories of his dad coaching his hockey team and both of them attending sporting events together. The best memory was of the first fishing trip he took with his dad one summer when he was just 9 or 10 years old. That memory had become a particularly special one as he grew into the man he was today. It has been and will always be a great memory for both him and his dad Byron.

2

Reminiscing

Byron woke from the surgery and the recovery prognosis was not great. Arthur was very happy to see his father opening his eyes and waking up, but unfortunately over the next couple of days he realized he was not the dad he was just a few days ago. Life can change in seconds. Sleep and rest was what Byron needed now. The doctors had told his family, Byron's recovery would take months and most likely years. Arthur knew his dad, had a strong will and would not give up on life without a fight.

Despite having a stroke and a brain surgery, it appeared to Arthur his father still had a good memory but had a little trouble speaking. Byron's speech was slower and sometimes he appeared to speak with a heavy accent, but he could be understood. Now, a day later, Arthur sat by his father's bed and watched with happiness and relief, as his father woke from sleeping and began to talk. Byron started reminiscing about an experience he had with his own father when he was just a boy. It seemed to Arthur that the medical condition had softened his dad.

"I was dreaming about a trip into the woods fishing with my dad, your grandfather," he said. Arthur said "you rest now dad," but his father kept talking in a low voice ignoring his son's advice. "I remember it, as if it was yesterday." Arthur appreciated the fact his father's memory was still good.

Byron's father had passed away when Byron was just thirteen years old. Byron started telling Arthur; "I remember my father saying, 'get ready, and let's go fishing at Hawkes Pond." The trail entrance into the woods to Hawkes pond was just a few minutes up the road from our house". "The walk to Hawkes Pond was a good hour and a half," Byron said. Arthur knew where his dad was talking about because Byron had pointed out the path entrance to Arthur many times, as the two drove by it. In fact, it was pointed out every time while driving through Creston South where Byron was born.

Byron continued, "I removed my bamboo fishing pole from where it was stored under our house, got on my hip rubbers and was ready to go." Byron had received his hip rubbers the month before, a rare treat to receive being one of 15 children. A luxury! "Dad had already dug some worms and packed a bag with necessities for the trip", he went on to say.

"That sure was a good day my son", Byron reminisced. Arthur could see his father was tired and needed to rest so he said, "I have to go find a nurse dad and will be right back. We can talk about this again later, okay dad?" Byron was tired but did not want his son to leave. Looking straight at Arthur, he nodded his head he said, "yes, okay my son."

Arthur left his father's bedside with mixed emotions. It was still early in the recovery, Arthur usually went to find a nurse whenever his father first woke up from sleeping. When Arthur returned with the nurse, Louise was already at his father's side, but Byron had already fallen back to sleep. "Your father needs some rest now, the nurse said,

I will check his vitals but it's best for you all to go home for some rest," Arthur waited for the nurse to confirm Byron's vitals were okay before he left his bedside. Louise stayed for many more hours with Byron before leaving to go home. During this time alone with Byron, she felt very alone. Louise got into bed behind him and hugged him close while she quietly wept. She had a heavy heart as she left Byron's bedside late that night to return home. The next day Arthur returned to find his father alone and much more alert but still confined to bed.

3

Walking Trail

A few days later, Arthur was at his dad's bedside when he said "okay dad now that you are feeling a little better, I'd like to hear more about the fishing story with grandfather". "Sure," said Byron. Byron was grateful for the opportunity to talk to his son, it helped distract him from everything health related.

"Well son, it was about mid-morning on that warm summer day, when Dad and I started out on our unplanned fishing trip".

The main road through Creston South was just a dirt road with loose gravel that had worked its way out of the soil and now lay on top of the road. The loose gravel had gradually worked its way to the road side because of foot and a little car traffic. There was also the occasional game of road hockey that moved the gravel around. The loose gravel was now built up a few centimeters on the road sides. There was not a lot of traffic in those days. The local people could not afford to buy large costly items like cars or trucks. Local folks did not have a lot of money and they did not like to borrow from a bank. The little money that was available was spent on life's necessities for their families. The priority had to be the family's needs, not wants."

My dad, your grandfather, Arch, was in the lead as we walked up Crocker's Lane. Crocker's Lane was a dirt side road, branched from the main road through town now named Crocker's Road. The lane was named Crocker's, because most of the land bordering the lane was owned by families of Crocker's for generations. Still, even now, most of the folks living on that road have the last name Crocker. We were all related in some way, cousins, aunts, uncles, 2nd cousins, generations of us. Dad and I walked along the lane and turned right onto the main road. I followed behind because my dad knew the trail to the pond much better than me. The two of us turned off the road onto the trail, and being young and with my dad, I was excited. The trail was sometimes dry and rocky but other times boggy with water holes and marsh. Sometimes I struggled to keep up. Occasionally your grandfather would stop to check on me and ask if I was okay.

Continuing hiking along for about an hour we came to a place named by locals, The Yellow Marsh. The marsh did have a greenish yellow tint across the top of it because of the vegetation that grew here. There were also patches of muddy bog. Dad told me "don't step into the mud bog areas, they're like quick sand and bottomless. once you step in, you do not return." I took great care to avoid the mud holes. Gradually we made our way across the marsh, and arrived at a brook called Grandfathers Brook. Dad stopped and said, 'We will have a little spell here my son'. We both searched and found a large rock to sit on for a rest."

I was enjoying this rare time sitting with my father at the edge of the brook on a warm day. I was curious, so I asked dad "Why is this place was named Grandfather's Brook?" Dad explained, 'Well my son, one time there was an old man who built a log cabin here that stood for many years. It survived long after he passed. The old cabin eventually fell into the ground and was just about all rotten and gone back to nature when I started to come this way as a boy with my father, your grandfather. There's nothing left of it now. Like everything made by men's hands, it will all disappear one day. Whatever is made with hands will one day come tumbling down, that's just the way it is my son."

The brook was about 2 meters wide at this point and shallow. It was easy to cross with our rubbers on. Looking up and down the brook, I could see the brook was overhung with trees and brush along its banks. I knew, just up the brook a few hundred meters there was a swimming hole that my friends and I had built by damming the brook with stones and other material from the brook banks and the wooded area. I often went here on hot summer days to wade and swim in the water with my friends.

Byron's Dad took a deep breath, and slowly let it out. Suddenly he stood up and said, "Okay, let's get moving my son." The two of us continued on up the trail and by late morning we had arrived at our destination, Hawks Pond.

4

Hawks Pond

Continuing on their journey, the pair arrived at Hawks Pond. Byron immediately had his mind on fishing. He looked out over the pond at the clear water. Not a cloud in the sky with the sun high above indicating it was near midday. A slight breeze from the south gave the appearance of diamonds dancing across the water. Just across the pond to his left Byron saw the old beaver's house that had been there for years. A few beavers were still residing in the pond. His eyes scanned the area around the pond. Among the tall trees was an area of smaller, shorter trees. New forest growth was springing up in the areas that had been cut by locals for firewood to burn in their stoves during the winter.

Byron and his father both had bamboo poles for fishing. Byron uncoiled his line from the pole, while his dad was building a fire to make lunch and tea, "a boil up" as his father called it. To use a bamboo fishing pole, took some ingenuity. The line was coiled around the pole the full length of it and the hook's sharp tip pushed into the pole at the base to hold everything tight and in place on the pole for carrying and storage. To use it, first the line had to be uncoiled from the pole. When the line was uncoiled Byron added a bobber about a meter from the hook attached to the end of the line and a 3 oz. lead sinker just above the hook. The bobber would alert him when a fish was biting at his hook. The sinker helped to set the hook full of bait deep into the water. The bobber and sinker also added some weight at the end of the fishing line, to make it easier to flick out into the water. In those days casting rods weren't available. If casting rods were available, the Crocker's did not own one. Bamboos were much cheaper and were more affordable for a family that did not have a lot of money.

To flick the line, the hook and the bobber, out into the pond took some skill. It had to be completed in one motion. The bamboo had to be held at its base with both hands and the pole held straight up high into the air with the line dangling freely. The pole then had to be motioned backward then suddenly lunged forward, all in one motion, with as much strength as one could muster. Fishing with a bamboo pole was an art-like process in itself. Fishing with a bamboo pole took practice to achieve the placing of the hook into the pond with precision, where a fisherman assumed there were fish. Byron had been using this method of fishing since first trying fishing a number of years earlier with his father and his brothers. Byron decided on a place to flick his hook and line out. With the fishing pole held tight and straight up into the air, the pole went in one motion backward and forward. Swoosh! Byron flicked the line out into the pond as far as possible in one fast motion. The flick out into the pond looked good to Byron. He then stood on the bank of the pond watching his bobber on the water surface for any sign of a trout. The bobber was made from cork material and colored red and white, making it easy to see on the water surface.

Arch had gone about starting a fire which was now burning very well. He had cut a tree branch, stuck it into the ground and placed it on an angle to lean over the fire. This branch would be used to hang the Billy Kettle to boil water to make tea. Byron kept glancing over at his dad, noticing his father was unpacking the food and cooking gear from his back sack. Arch removed the lightweight frying pan first and placed it to straddle the fire on the stones he had set up in the right position to hold the frying pan. He then added some butter to the frying pan. As it began to melt he added bologna. In the quiet of the morning Byron could hear the bologna sizzle as it cooked under his father's watchful eye. As the smell of cooking filled the air Bryon thought, "Man that smells good." "Okay my son get a plate and I'll give you a slice", his dad said. Byron grabbed a pate and watched as his dad added the bologna plus a slice of homemade bread with butter and molasses. "Eat that, it'll grow hair on your chest my son," Arch said with a grin. "When that's gone we will make tea" as he filled his own plate with food.

Byron found a dry place to sit. Lunch was delicious, nothing like bread, molasses and fried bologna on a fishing trip. The molasses had soaked the bread and it stuck to his fingers as he ate it. Here they were father and son sitting on the banks of Hawks Pond, with a fire burning and lunch in hand. Life was slowed down. "It doesn't get any better than this my son," his dad said

Arch finished eating and stood up, "okay my son, time to get some water for the kettle. take the kettle over there, where the brook runs into the pond, running water is best to boil, for tea," Arch stated, pointing towards a small stream running into the pond.

Byron promptly went to fill the kettle and returned quickly. He knew his dad enjoyed a cup of tea right after eating. Arch took the kettle and hung it on the branch he had set up to allow the kettle to hang directly over the flame. He removed his pipe from his shirt pocket and filled it with Sail Pipe tobacco. He then picked up a piece of a branch laying on the ground. Arch reached into the fire with it and set it on fire just at the end to light his pipe as he puffed on it. He had brought his pipe along exactly for this occasion. He puffed away as both of them watched the tobacco smoke rise upward as he inhaled and exhaled. Byron liked the smell of the pipe smoke that filled the air. It was familiar. "I will do that when I get bigger" thought Byron. He then said to his dad," I think I would like to try that when I am older Dad."

Byron said turning to his son sitting on his hospital bed, "Well Arthur, your grandfather seemed surprised at my words." Dad told me, 'Don't take up smoking my son, it is expensive and not good for your lungs, I have been smoking since I was 9 years old, soon after I started my first job."

Byron continued to tell Arthur what his dad, Arch, had told him. "Your grandfather Arch explained, "came for me in school one day. I was sitting at my desk, when a knock was heard on the schoolhouse door. It was my father Eli, your grandfather, asking the school master to send me out, he wanted to talk to me. He had come to tell me, he had found me a job, paying five cents an hour and I was to leave school immediately and come with him. No, was not an answer any parent would accept in those days. The word 'no' to a parent was not an option that could be considered. It was hard times then," Arch said, looking out into the pond as if he was thinking about that day his father took him out of school to go to work. Then in a low tone of voice as if in regret he said "Byron, those were hard times my son, I would not wish it on you. My father was responsible to ensure the family was taken care of and it was the job of sons to help in any way he thought necessary to help the family. I had two sisters who helped mom with the house chores, but us three boys had many chores to perform daily especially in summer, plus a paying job if we were lucky enough to have one."

In summer we had to tend gardens and animals,. We also had to help dad ensure fire wood was available for the winter. We owned two horses, a herd of sheep and about a hundred hens It was hard to know exactly how many hens we had because we had kill them for for our Sunday dinners. The animals were not pets. In the garden we grew potatoes, carrots, cabbage, parsnips, turnips and beets. They were all harvested in the fall. Some vegetables were used to make jarred goods such as relish and pickled beets, while most was stored in the root cellar for winter use. We also had to help cut and store the hay for the horse for winter. As we got older we went fishing with dad as he needed help, especially with the catching of cod and the splitting of the cod to salt and dry."

Then just as if to avoid any more of those thoughts, thoughts that reminded him of a more difficult life behind him, Arch said "okay Byron let's make tea, enough of the talking of times back then, the water is almost ready to boil," as he reached into a bag. The bag held loose Red Rose tea he had brought with him, commonly referred to as pound tea. Red Rose tea was the most popular tea used in most homes in Newfoundland. Arch took a handful of the dry tea and gently placed it into the kettle that was now steaming, ready to boil in a minute or two. Byron's father sat down and was enjoying his pipe. He looked out across the pond, probably remembering the days visiting this pond with his own dad and the times he came here to cut wood with his older son's, Byron's older brothers.

Byron went over to the fire to remove the kettle. Suddenly he heard his father's voice shout words of caution. "Let it boil over twice before you remove it from the fire. "Wait a few minutes", he said, "We will have a great cup of tea". Byron, knowing his dad knew best, just stepped back from the fire and said, "Okay dad I'll wait a little while". Byron waited for the boiling water to settle down then boil again over the side of the kettle. With his father's approving nod Byron reached in to remove the boiling kettle of steaming hot tea from the fire. As Byron laid the kettle to the side, his father stood up to pour the tea into the tin mugs he had removed from his back pack earlier. "Okay dad, let's drink the tea and get fishing," Byron stated in a matter of fact tone of voice. "Yes! Let's do that my son." Arch said.

The pair drank their tea and finished eating the food they had taken with them from home. Although there was fried bologna, and bread with molasses, (bread made by Bryon's mother from scratch, no store bought back then), there were no sweets. It was a great day for father and son bonding.

After finishing eating and packing up, it was time to start fishing again. The pair were enjoying the pond as they occasionally changed fishing areas, gradually moving around the edge of the pond. Around mid-afternoon, after they had reached the opposite side of the pond from where they started, Arch stopped to make a fire again for what he told Byron was for a very special afternoon mug up. Arch gathered some twigs and small wood. In no time at all he had a fire burning. "Okay my son," he said, "prepare for the special ingredient." Arch told Byron to fill up the Billy Kettle with water and ready it onto the fire to boil. Within a few minutes the Billy kettle was on the fire and the water was steaming. While the water was starting to boil, he reached into his bag and removed a piece of dried salt cod fish and some brown paper bags. "Yuk" Byron whispered under his breath. His dad then wrapped the salted dried cod fish in the paper. After the kettle had boiled over for the second time. Arch said "Okay take the kettle from the fire," motioning to Byron to lay the kettle of water on the ground near the fire. His dad then laid the wrapped fish onto the ambers of the fire and watched as the paper burned around it turning the fish black. He then removed the fish and placed the fish inside the kettle. "Okay Byron," he said, "we will let that soak in there for a few minutes before we eat it." You have a few flicks while we wait," Arch told Byron. "Okay dad," he replied.

After about twenty minutes, Arch yelled, "Okay my son let's eat". The thought of that fish was not appetizing to Byron, at all. Byron's father took a chunk from the fish in the pot and gave it to Byron, taking the rest of the fish and placing it on a plate for himself along with a slice of homemade bread and butter. He looked at Byron and said "Just take the fish and wrap it in the bread and butter like this", as he wrapped some fish inside his piece of bread. "Man, that's some good, it'll make you grow big and strong", he said, as he took a big bite and chewed it. Byron followed his father's lead and wrapped his fish inside the bread he had. As soon as Byron bit down and began to chew, he tasted just the salt and burned fish. His first instinct was to spit it out, but did not because his dad was so convinced the meal would make him grow big and strong. "Not bad dad', Byron said without revealing his true thoughts. "I told you my son that is good," Arch explained.

Byron was not listening because he was already wondering how long it would be before he would be getting big and strong, like his father told him. Byron admitted to himself the fish did not seem so bad with a mouthful of the tea his father made. He started to like it more as he ate. The combination of the buttered bread, the soaked salty fish and the tea made him feel like a real grown up, maybe even his father's favorite son.

Soon the mug up was finished, the dishes washed in the pond and packed into the backpack Arch re-lite his pipe of unfinished tobacco left from earlier in the day and they went back to fishing.

They continued fishing for the next couple of hours. Fishing with a bamboo pole was not an easy feat for a young boy like Byron, but he had done well, catching a dozen trout and placing them on a Y branch he had cut from an alder tree. He had just put the final catch on the Y-branch through the gills and mouth for ease of carrying, when he heard his father say, "Okay, my son get your trout and pole ready and let's head home, your mother will have supper ready by the time we get there.

5

Red Harbour Falls

Byron's massive stroke had required brain surgery to remove blood clots in his brain. He was paralyzed on his left side for now and would need further care at the rehabilitation center located in the south end of Halifax.

For the next ninety days Arthur would be his father's evening companion. During Arthur's visits they talked about many things; family matters, sports and especially their fond memory of a fishing trip they had to Red Harbour Falls when Arthur was just a boy. Arthur's first big fishing trip with his father.

Arthur had heard his father talk about Red Harbour Falls Ponds many times long before he was invited by his dad to come along on his first big fishing trip.

From his hospital bed in the Rehab Centre, Bryon continued to explain and reminisce about Red Harbour Falls.

The small fishing village of Red Harbour, is located about 20 km's down the highway from the town of Marystown. Some of Arthur's relatives still live and work there, making a living from the sea.

The actual town of Red Harbour, is located just down river from the Red Harbour Highway Bridge and located near where the river empties into the ocean bay of Placentia Bay. The main source of employment at the time of Bryon's early years was inshore fishing.

Byron's sister (Arthur's Aunt Millie) and family had floated their house from Flat Island to Red Harbor. The Newfoundland government initiated a resettlement program to move folks from remote areas of Newfoundland including the many islands dotted around Placentia Bay to the main island of Newfoundland. Many other families also floated their homes to Red Harbour in hopes of continuing a life they knew, making a living from the sea. A life that continues for many up to the present. Millie passed away in recent years and her husband is a retire senior now and still lives there. Two of their three sons and family still live in Red Harbor and depend on the sea to make a living.

Most families in this small out port town of Red Harbour, own a fishing boat while others are employed at businesses located in Marystown, the biggest town located on the Burin Peninsula on the south coast of Newfoundland. As the ability to make a living from the sea diminishes many younger folks, unable or unwilling to carry on the fishing life of their forefathers are moving away in hopes of finding a better life. Eventually this town may have only retired seniors living here. but for now it is doing okay. A similar story is being played out . in many over towns that make up out port Newfoundland.

Red Harbour welcomes you by a single two way traffic road with wood houses of different colors speckled along its side. Although some new houses have been built over the years most of the houses here were floated into the town from islands dotted around Placentia Bay, just like Aunt Millie's house was. The single two way traffic road continues for about 5 km and ends at the harbours shore, where the ocean washes the land. It is at this point the Red Harbour river empties its pristine contents into the Atlantic ocean waters of Placentia

Bay. Newfoundlanders refer to these areas where the ocean meets the land affectionately as "the land wash". (Where the ocean washes the land).

Located on the shoreline of the harbour are the fisherman's wharves, which are multipurpose. Here fishermen build a shack to mend nets, store gear, unload their catch, and work on their boats. Fishermen also use these wharves for boarding and onboarding boats of any supplies or equipment. The wharf posts are embedded into the ground of the land wash area, while others are embedded just a few meters out into the ocean floor to increase the wharf size, making them structurally sound. . Many recycled tires are strategically hung by a cable or rope from the wharf top, to just above water level. The tires cushion the boats snuggling up against the wharves. Local fishermen tie up their boats here during evenings, overnights and days during the fishing season when the winds and water make it too rough to fish. . Nets can also be unloaded and placed in the shacks, dotted along the wharfs, for mending. The fishing shacks are seldom locked. Locks are for honest folks. A criminal will break locks to get at whatever they think they want to steal.

Looking out toward the ocean, are a few colorful boats on moorings. Looking past these boats, is the vastness of the ocean as far as the eye can see. One can see and hear the turbulent ocean as waves break onto the shore. The narcissistic ocean is constantly calling your eyes back to its beauty and restlessness. Even when a person looks away the ocean calls you back to hear its roar and gaze at it one more time. The ocean keeps reminding us, "listen to my roar, and admire my beauty". Standing near the edge of the ocean a person feels calm, peaceful, but also in awe. Red Harbour is such a place.

6

Dreams And Hopes

It was June 1989, Arthur had just finished the school year. He was in the kitchen, grabbing a snack, when he heard his dad talking on the phone with his friend Jack Phillimore. They were planning a fishing trip to Red Harbour falls for the next day, early morning as usual.

As he listened to his father, a thought entered the young boy's mind, "maybe this time I'll get to go!" He felt the excitement go through his body, with just the thought of the possibility of going to Red Harbour Falls Pond on a fishing trip with his Dad and Jack. The rest of the day and evening went by, with a hopeful little boy dreaming and wishing Even though his dad had not mentioned a thing. Arthur had expectations!

The night passed with Arthur having a restless sleep, waking twice during the night believing he had heard his dad waking him up to go fishing. He realized they were only dreams. Disappointed, Arthur continued his restless sleep.

Early the next morning Arthur heard his dad getting up and Jack arriving in the driveway, tooting the horn of his SUV and then he heard them drive away. The house felt empty, he felt the pain of disappointment as he lay in his bed. He was happy to be alone because nobody could see the tears of discouragement fall down his cheeks as he lay in bed. He wondered if his dad knew how he felt. He had wanted to go fishing so badly and was hoping for what he thought would be the miracle of dad taking him along. He had even prayed about it, in his bedtime prayers last night, just as his parents taught him. His mom Agnes and dad Byron would, before tucking him into bed at night, taught him to kneel to say prayers. He knew God didn't answer prayer immediately because "sometimes God listens to prayer, "his mom said, "but takes a little time to answer, in God's time, not ours." Arthur had been saying his prayers every night since he was able to talk. So, Arthur thought, "not this time dad, but I will go with you soon for sure", and then spoke in a loud voice "right God?" as if to convince God of what was the right thing to do.

Arthur, during his boyhood years, had heard many fishing stories about fishing in Red Harbour Falls Ponds while listening to conversations between his dad, Jack, his Uncle Nick and Uncle Bob, in the summer around a campfire, but especially in the winter months while they sat around the wood stove. To him Red Harbour Falls had taken on the appearance of a mystical place in his day and night dreams, probably because he had heard so many great and sometimes funny fishing stories about it. He wanted so badly to fish with his father, to experience the place for himself.

It was summer. Daylight until almost 10 P.M. About 7 P.M. Jack dropped Byron off in the driveway. Jack noticed Arthur and in a serious tone he said, "Arthur, my boy, pretty soon you will be old enough and big enough to go fishing at Red Harbour Falls with your father and I." Arthur's heart skipped a beat at the thought and he laughed a nervous laugh and said "that would be great." Arthur's dad then said "soon maybe, after he grows a little older and taller, maybe by the end of this summer, but for sure by next spring or summer". At that Arthur's heart sank a little with disappointment but he was sure he had grown a little taller in seconds. Arthur, for his age, was not a big boy, at nine years old.

Jack was a big man, about 220 pounds, at least 6 ft. Tall, bald, broad shoulders, muscular and strong, but not overweight. He always seemed upbeat, smiling or laughing. Arthur did not remember a time when Jack actually had hair. Jack had been bald since his early twenties long before Arthur came to know him.

Arthur and his father's friend Jack were hockey fans who cheered for the Toronto Maple Leaf's. Jack and his wife Jean had come to his family home many Saturday nights to watch Hockey Night in Canada broadcast on the Canadian Broadcasting Corporation (CBC), with his parents. He was usually allowed to stay up to watch the hockey game when his favorite team, the Toronto Maple Leaf's were playing, until he fell asleep. When he fell asleep his father would carry him to his bedroom, and tuck him in bed without Arthur waking. Arthur never did remember being carried off to bed or tucked in by his dad. The next day Arthur remembered the hockey game as far as the time sleep had overtaken him. Sometimes while Arthur was in bed, during the hockey game, he would be woken up to the cheers of his mom, dad, Jack and Jean, cheering a goal or a win for the Leaf's. The Leaf's winning didn't happen often in his boyhood years! The next morning at breakfast, he always inquired about the hockey game score, wanting to hear that Toronto had won, but it wasn't often. The fact was they rarely won at this time in the Leaf's history. Arthur's father always made the joke; "I have included the Leaf's team in my will to ask them to be my pallbearers. That way they can let me down one last time". Byron was losing faith in the Leaf's ever winning the Stanley Cup again, as were many other fans but not Arthur. His young imagination had not yet left him. Unfortunately children lose their imagination as they grow into adults.

In June that year, his parents registered him to play baseball in the local kid's league, but Arthur was not an athlete. He usually played hockey during the winter because his dad coached Arthur's team in the local rink novice division or whatever hockey division he was playing in. Arthur loved to play sports for fun and enjoyed the friendship of his teammates.

When Arthur was just three or four years old, his papa taught him to skate on the frozen salt water cove just behind his house in Mortier Bay. Arthur's Grandfather also went at least once weekly to the local arena for skating with him and his dad. Arthur and his papa had a special relationship. His grandfather talked to him like he was a grown up already and he liked that.

Grandfather had also taught him, when he was just three or four years old, how to drive nails with a hammer. At that age the hammer was almost too heavy for him to lift, but as the days went by, he got stronger and better at driving nails straight into the wood.

Summer was a great time in Arthur's life, doing things as a family and with his friends. He enjoyed the days without school. Billy and Arthur have been neighbors and best friends since he moved from The Basin to Bakes cove to live in the renovated papa's house after his papa passed.

Billy was much taller and bigger than Arthur, but then his parents were both like giants to Arthur. In the summer they spent a lot of their waking hours outside doing stuff together and being buddies. The two often went to the local shallow brook, Hynes Brook. They built a hangout cabin in the forest near the brook, learning to use only an axe or a saw, and a hammer, not an easy task for young boys. They used whatever tools they could get from their parents. The boys spent time scouting out, finding and carrying any available board from around the neighborhood to include in their plans of building their "hang out" cabin. Their allowances were spent buying nails for the planned build. Sometimes they removed nails from scrap boards around the neighborhood which they stored in an old empty tin can at the cabin location to use as needed.

The boy's parents were not aware of the camp building but knew they disappeared for many hours a day working on something. Another young man Denny also became their friend and took part in the camp building. Denny's grandfather had a saw mill for sawing logs into lumber. The slabs by-product of the logs were ripe for the boys to remove from the mills scrap wood pile with Denny's grandfather's permission. The discarded bark cover log exteriors were referred to as slabs. .It took some time and ingenuity as the boys carried as many of these slabs into the forest to the cabin building site. The slabs were moved by hand, wagons and carts. The boys took as many as they thought would be needed. Denny's grandfather was happy the boys were removing the slabs. The boys put the slabs to good use and Denny's grandfather was glad he did not have to discard them.

Even though the wheels of time have sent them in different directions the boys have remained friends.

That summer, waiting to go on that illusive fishing trip to Red Harbour Falls with his dad in his head, Arthur tried to eat food that would make him grow stronger and taller, even vegetables that he did not like. He knew how constantly working at something, like building a camp, made him stronger and better. He was determined to be invited to go on his long awaited fishing trip by summer's end.

7

Too Soon

It was September and Arthur had already started back to school for the new school year when he heard his dad planning the last fishing trip for the summer with Jack. Byron's plan was to go to the Red Harbour Falls the upcoming Saturday. Arthur's thought "maybe this time dad will take me". It would probably be the last trout fishing trip for the summer. He made sure his responsibilities around the house and yard were being taken care of as much as possible so his dad would notice and possibly think he deserved a special reward, like going fishing with him and Jack on Saturday.

It was late Friday afternoon about an hour after Byron had arrived home from his job, he noticed Arthur and said, "come here let's have a little chat. Arthur, you know Jack and I are going fishing in the morning." The boy's heart skipped a beat, and he thought, maybe this was it, he was going also, this time. Then his dad touched him on the head gently and quietly said, "I noticed you did a great job around the house this past week, but I do think Red Harbour Falls is too long and difficult a walk for you yet my son, especially the climb up around the falls to the ponds." Arthur felt the pain of the disappointment deep inside his heart and stomach. Then his father stated the words that he had been waiting to hear forever. Byron looked at his son and said, "I promise as soon as school finishes in June next year, you can come fishing with Jack and me to Red Harbour Falls Ponds."

June seemed so far away but it made Arthur excited just realizing he was definitely going trout fishing next summer and probably many more days after that. He felt confident because he knew his dad always kept his promises.

8

The Uncles

Arthur had neighbor's with the surname of wetly who had a brilliant dog named Tesh. Tesh was not a pure breed, she was just a mutt, a Heinz 57 as locals referred to her. Tesh always came over to Arthur's yard for some play time and they grew closer as time went on.

One summer day Arthur was playing second baseman in the local kid's baseball league. It was about mid game when suddenly Tesh ran out on the field with a rock in her mouth, ran over to him and dropped it at his feet, wanting him to play toss and fetch. All the fans, mostly parents and relatives sitting in the stands, were laughing. Arthur just gave Tesh a pat and rub and said, "I can't do that now Tesh, but we can later'. Tesh seemed to understand as she ran off the field and disappeared at least until the game ended. Tesh appeared again at the end of the game. She seemed to know it was over and followed Arthur home for some play time. Tesh was one of his best friends that summer. There's nothing like the friendship between a boy and a dog.

Arthur remembered one summer evening his parents had a BBQ

with some family and friends invited to their house. Arthur's Uncle Austin got his steak from the BBQ and laid it on a plate placed on the patio picnic table and went inside for a moment to get the side dishes he preferred. While Austin was inside getting his side dishes, he just happened to look out the window to see Tesh grab his steak and run off. There was a little laughter by everyone over this happening, but not Austin. Arthur couldn't understand his Uncle's anger, because Tesh most likely was hungry.

Tesh kept him in great company that summer, but as summer was coming to an end, Arthur still had not received his most wanted and most hoped for invite; from his dad to go to Red Harbour Falls Pond to fish. He was getting very concerned.

One night Arthur's twin Uncles, Robert (Bob) and Nick came for a visit. As usual the conversation amongst all the men turned to fishing. It began with a story about their first visit to Red Harbour Falls. A few Years ago on his dad's very first time there his Uncle Bob said he had gone and knew the way. This was news to his Uncle Nick! So they started planning a fishing trip with Bob, to a spot just above Red Harbour Falls. Uncle Bob was anxious to have a day of trout fishing, exploring and showing the other two where he used to go.

Uncle Nick and Bob arrived to get Byron, early morning in Nick's car. Off they went, heading out for Bob's fishing spot as he had remembered. As they approached the town of Red Harbour, Bob directed Nick to turn left off the highway and continue on an old dirt and gravel side road that was barely usable. This was once the main road, but it was abandoned when the new highway was built. It hadn't been used for a long time. Nick followed the road to an old bridge made from concrete that looked stable enough to drive over, then drove a few more kilometers until Bob said, "This is where we need to park and find the footpath down to the Red Harbour River." Following Bob's directions they continued to walk the trail to the river with Bob leading the way.

They arrived at the river bank where they saw a fast flowing river that was usually only frequented by salmon fisherman, when the season was open. The trio continued to walk along the river bank, with Bob's directions, leading the way. At times they had to walk out into the river to escape tree branches and large boulders. After walking for about an hour they approached a Y in the river. The river was flowing toward them from two directions. The river had branched into two fast flowing tributaries of the Red Harbour River. Byron and Nick looked to Bob for direction. Bob motioned with his hands as he walked forward and said "this way boys" and led the way as they continued their trek. After walking another hour Byron and Nick got concerned they were not going in the right direction. "Is this the wrong way?" Bob knelt down, placed his ear on the ground and insisted he could hear the falls, proving it was the right direction. Byron and Nick just laughed.

Bob insisted on going forward, promising they would soon be at their destination. Nick didn't want to argue with his twin brother, but teased Bob just a little. Although skeptical, the pair kept following Bob, because they did not know the location of Red Harbour Falls or the ponds, but seriously doubted they'd find it today. Hiking along, concern continued to creep in about Bob finding the falls. They had walked for another hours when all three realized Bob had taken them in the wrong direction at the area where the river had branched.

After following the river for a long time, the river started to meander and its flow was really slowing. Byron said 'I think we have arrived close to the river headwaters". All agreed! After a short discussion it was decided to make a fire and have a mug up (Newfoundland slang for lunch) to talk about their next plan. After boiling the water in the Billy kettle to make tea, they all had a mug up of a few sandwiches, tea and some sweets they had brought. A Billy kettle is a kettle fashioned from a large juice can with the lid removed and wire for a hanger to hang the kettle over the fire to boil the water. While eating, joking and laughing they decided to turn inland and walk up on a hill to check for any nearby ponds. After finding a pond, but not the river falls they were looking for, they fished a while and caught a few trout, but not many. They teased Bob and said, "It was a long walk without much to show for it." The hike was a good day out for male bonding and great fun. They decided it was time to head home to ensure they got home before dark.

Uncle Bob took a lot of sarcastic barbs from Nick and Byron on the two and a half hour walk down the river and back to the car for the 20 kilometer drive home. Bob still gets kidded about it even now. At the time Bob said, maybe he would never live it down, it was embarrassing indeed. "I did eventually take you guys to Red Harbor Falls Ponds fishing though boys," said Bob. "You sure did," said his brother Nick.

After hearing the story amongst the men Arthur thought, maybe the hike to Red Harbour Falls Pond would be too difficult of a walk for him at his size and age. They didn't own an ATV, not many people in the town did. ATV's were too expensive. Arthur was starting to realize why his dad thought he was not ready to go up the Red Harbour River to the special fishing place just yet, but he said nothing, other than laugh at their story. He didn't want to admit it to his dad it was possibly to big a journey for him. Their stories did not deter Arthur though. Arthur was still determined to go with his dad fishing to that special place. Just the thought of going on that fishing trip with his dad excited him. He knew he could do it. Arthur also knew that if there were areas that were too difficult for him to access, his father or Jack could carry him or help him along

9

Hockey Creats Memories

Soon the fall turned colder. Fall is a beautiful time of year as the leaves lose their green, turning to yellow, orange and red before dropping to the ground. Winter soon was upon Arthur's home town. During the fall he registered to play minor hockey, a sport he really liked.

His father had registered himself to play in the recreational hockey league and his sister for figure skating. Both he and his sister were registered for piano lessons. Arthur liked the piano lessons, not because he liked the piano, the lessons gave him the opportunity to socialize with his aunt and her daughter, his cousin. It was obvious to his parents that his interest was miniscule at best, so his aunt suggested to his mother to remove him from lessons. That was the end of that. Madison was doing great and eventually registered with the Royal Conservatory for further training, where she reached level eight, before her interest waned.

Byron decided to coach Arthur's minor league hockey. It just made sense. Might as well coach the team if he was going to all the practices and games anyway, no matter the time or place. However, Byron did not give his son any preferences. Arthur actually thought his father was harder on him, probably trying not to show any biases. Arthur was not the easiest to get out of bed at 6:30 A.M. Saturday mornings for hockey practice or a game, but Byron was having none of it. He got Arthur up, dressed in some of his hockey gear and ready for the rink. Many of those mornings were oh so cold. Together they dressed warm after eating a good breakfast his dad had prepared; eggs, bacon and toast, and they were on their way. Occasionally Arthur just wanted cereal for breakfast but his dad insisted on a good hot breakfast in their belly. "It's best to play hockey with a good breakfast in your stomach," he often said "and it will be hours before we will get a chance to eat again."

Arthur was a good skater for his age, but he could not carry the puck and pass very well. He did not know what to do with the puck, his dad said. Arthur needed lots of practice. Arthurs skating skills were good, because of his papa (grandfather). His papa would take him out onto the frozen saltwater cove near his house to give him skating tips from the time he was one years old. He also went to public skating with his family about once a week. Sometimes his papa would also tag along. At least once a week after school their babysitter took both Arthur and his sister Madison to the local rink for skating.

Whether Arthur had the puck skills or not, he really enjoyed the game. Occasionally his father took his sister Madison along to the rink to watch him play hockey Arthur's good friends Jimmy and Billy occasionally came to watch, but did not play hockey. Arthur convinced Billy to give it a try. A few years later as a teen, Billy decided to play hockey in position of goalie.

When Arthur and his dad arrived at the rink, often some other kids were already there with one parent. Byron got the key from the rink attendant and opened a dressing room that was usually warm, when the rink was cold. All the boys soon filled the dressing room area and started to get into the remainder of their hockey gear and skates. It seemed getting on the skates and lacing them up was a big chore for the boys. The parents that were around usually helped with this. All the chatter made the dressing room noisy, with a parent yelling occasionally for them to be quiet. But the camaraderie among the group was invigorating before they got on the ice.

Some parents dropped off their kids and just left, returning later, usually close to the end of the game. That behavior really seemed to irritate Arthur's father because he thought the parents should stay to support their children.

Byron noticed during the games some kids would look up into the arena seats to check if a parent was there. When the young boys saw their parents it made them much happier and it gave them the energy to play harder.

Byron often thought of the quote by Theodor Seuss Geisel, "Sometimes a parent does not realize the value of a moment until it's a moment of a memory missed".

10

Christmas

    Christmas came quickly. Arthur and Madison were making their gift list known to their parents. As usual their parents listened but were non–committal about any present possibilities. All the local kids looked forward to Christmas with anticipation. At school the chatter was always about what everybody was hoping to get for Christmas gifts.

    Finally the big day before Christmas day arrived, Christmas Eve. Arthur and Madison were sent to bed about 9:30 P.M. and had a very difficult time getting to sleep. All they could think about was Santa Claus and the presents that would be under their Christmas tree in the morning. After what seemed like hours of nervous anticipation sleep eventually came.

    The family Christmas tree had its own story this year: Arthur and Madison both lived with their mom and dad in a house once belonging to Madison and Arthur's Grandparents, Heber and Amy. During the winter it was cold living this close to the water especially when the winter's North East wind blew up the bay. But the great thing about the house was in winter the water in the cove froze over and Madison and Arthur could ice skate any day they wanted if it was not snowy or stormy outside. After a snowfall the local parents and kids all got together to clear an area for their kids to skate and play.

As usual during this time of year the whole family was planning and preparing for the Christmas season and a visit from Santa Claus. Agnes started her baking early. Baking her traditional dark fruit cake and many types of Christmas cookies. She kept them fresh for Christmas by placing them in the freezer. The Christmas delicacies were always shared with any relatives and friends that would visit during the Christmas season.

Then about a week before Christmas Eve on a sunny cold winter Saturday morning after a light snowfall, Madison heard her Dad ask her brother if he wanted to go with him and their dog Barry to cut a Christmas tree in the nearby forest. Madison was just a little girl (both in size and age), but she asked her father if she could also come along to help cut and bring home the Christmas tree. Byron smiled and said, "Well, if you dress up warm and put on your winter boots. It's cold and there is light snow on the ground." Madison got out her pink snowsuit, her warm pink winter boots, pink woolen mittens with strings and pink woolen hat that mom had purchased at a local craft fair just a few weeks earlier (she was all girl!) After getting himself ready to go, Madison's dad helped her get dressed. First he pulled on her boots then placed the mittens on a string over her shoulders and across the back of her neck, down each arm, hidden by the snow suit, which allowed them to be worn on the hands without getting lost. When the pink mittens were not on her hands they dangled on the string at her fingertips. The snow suit covered the top of her boots, not allowing snow to get inside to melt and make her feet cold. She was prepared!

Although her father helped her get dressed, Madison was very independent for her age and said, "I can do it myself". Her dad said "I know you can, but I want to get going so I am helping you just to speed things up".

Arthur got dressed quickly and was soon waiting in the car. Shortly after Madison joined him. Byron buckled Madison into her seat, next to Barry the dog, who was already in the car and sitting on the back seat. Together Byron, Arthur and Madison all drove off to cut a Christmas tree in the nearby forest. The smile on their face was priceless. It was so exciting! People in Arthur and Madison's home town did not buy a tree for Christmas. They went to cut their own in one of the many wooded areas located near town.

Today they drove to what was referred to as the back highway, a road near the forest not far from home. Byron found a safe place to park near a footpath that led into a wooded area near a brook. Arthur and his dad got out of the car. Arthur started into the forest following the footpath while his father was getting Madison out of the car. Arthur knew this area well because he and his friends had built a camp just a little further up the brook just last summer. Byron yelled at Arthur to wait until he was ready. Barry was really excited just jumping and running around. Byron pulled on Madison's pink mittens and pink wool cap, he pulled on his own gloves and cap and told Arthur to pull his mitts on also. Finally they were on their way. Byron walked first, Madison followed second and third was Arthur. Byron looked at Arthur and said "keep an eye on your sister, buddy." Madison was just a little girl whose legs were not very tall yet, so she struggled to keep up, as the dog Barry ran around her and jumped up licking her face showing his happiness with her being along with them. The dogs activity made Madison giggle.

Although there was not much snow on the ground it was half way to Madison's knees. The light fluffy snow made it harder for her to walk. Byron's heart filled with joy, pride and love when he looked back often to check on her. He noticed her mittens were now dangling at her fingertips, as usual. Madison was just picking up snow in her bare hands to eat it. "We have to get those mittens on your hands honey," Byron said. Madison was so happy to be out with her brother and dad to find a Christmas tree, that she did not feel the cold on her hands. Her cheeks were rosy pink due to the frost biting at her cheeks. The wool cap kept falling forward and covering her eyes. She had to constantly raise her hand to push it back away from her eyes. The cold made her nose run, which it often did when outside on cold winter days. The dog licked her face once and a while and seemed to be worried about her.

Madison had a smile across her face that was a picture of pure happiness as she walked through the almost knee deep very light dry snow that had fallen. Dad offered to hold her hand but she refused. "I want to walk myself", she said, "Miss independent you are ", replied her dad. Arthur and his dad slowed to walk beside her, but soon her brother was walking ahead.

Barry ran to Arthur then back to Byron and Madison. After a while of walking so slow her father scooped up Madison and carried her in his arms and walked deeper into the forest. As Byron lay Madison back to the ground, he said, "We will need to find a tall tree that reaches the ceiling so we can have enough space to place all the presents from Santa Clause under it." Barry stayed with Madison wagging his tail, as the trio separately went weaving around trees looking to find a suitable Christmas tree. Madison started looking for a tree on her own with Barry by her side. Byron soon found what could be a suitable tree and shouted, "Come here you guys." Byron asked his children, "Do you two think this is a good tree for us?" Madison and Arthur yelled together, "It's tall and beautiful." Byron got the saw ready to cut the tree. As he was cutting the tree, Madison decided she wanted to help. Byron let her help, by placing one of her hands onto the handle of the saw. Snow was falling from the tree branches as they were cutting it. The snow fell down over their head, onto their faces and down their neck causing them to laugh as they continued cutting the tree.

Suddenly Byron stepped back and told Arthur to finish the job. "My son, if you plan to go fishing with Jack and I next summer to Red Harbour Falls, show me what you can do." Arthur jumped in to finish cutting the tree and watched with pride as he saw the tree fall to the ground. With the tree down, Madison decided she wanted to help her brother and father drag their Christmas tree back to the car.

It was a slow walk back to the car dragging the tree with Madison holding and pulling on one of the branches. She was proud she was helping pull it along (at least in her own mind!). Being siblings she and her brother argued about pulling the tree. Arthur was a little irritated about the slow progress, but Byron scolded him, to take his time because his sister was only little. They all eventually got back to the car. Once everyone was inside the car Byron turned on the heater to keep the children warm while he secured the tree to the car. He placed the tree onto the roof of the station wagon and fastened it down.

On their way home with the family evergreen Christmas tree, there were huge smiles on the faces of both the children. Madison was so proud of herself for helping to find and cut the family Christmas tree this year. "We needed a big tree to have room for all of the presents from Santa", Madison shouted from the back seat. "We sure do honey," her dad said.

When they arrived home Madison and Arthur ran into the house to tell their mom to come outside to have a look at the Christmas tree they had found. Agnes loved the tree and said, "Let's bring it inside later, but before we can decorate it your father has to remove the snow, cut it the right length and lay it on the porch to let it dry for a few hours." Byron went about getting the tree ready and placed it on the porch to dry. Madison and Arthur went to the porch many times that afternoon to check on their tree's progress of drying.

Later that afternoon Byron brought the tree into the living room and placed it in front of the living room window as Madison and Arthur proudly looked on and supervised.

Byron placed the tree into its final Christmas position and added the colored Christmas lights. Agnes turned to Madison and Arthur and said "it's time for you two to put your own tree ornaments on your tree!" They both felt so proud. Their mom got all the tree ornaments from storage as they looked on with anticipation while their dad made hot chocolate for all. It was only after the family was comfortable with their hot chocolate in hand and Christmas music was filling the air, did Agnes hand the two precious ornaments over to her children. Placing ornaments on the tree first, was a family Christmas tradition. The child who hung their ornament first was based on year born and Christmas year. Arthur who was born in 1979 went first in odd number years and Madison who was born in 1982 went first in even numbered years. As with family tradition, this being an even number year, it was Madison who first placed an ornament on the tree as her family clapped and shouted words of praise and encouragement, then rotated to Arthur who hung his ornament with clapping and words of encouragement and praise as well.

Madison and Arthur would continue hanging their personal ornaments on the tree late into their teen years. After leaving home, their mother gave their ornaments to them to hang on their own Christmas trees. Both of them still have their special ornament to hang on their own Christmas tree every year.

The tradition continues to this day with Madison's daughter, Ireland, who has her own Christmas ornament to hang on her Christmas tree, a crystal bell her (papa) Byron gave her at age two.

11

Traditions

After a night of restless sleep, Christmas morning arrived for Arthur and Madison. It was early morning and still dark outside as they crept down the stairs to the living room. Looking into the living room they could not contain their excitement, as they saw many presents under their Christmas tree. "Could all of this be ours?" they whispered to each other with wide eyed imagination, amazement and glee.

The rule was; if there were lights were on in any other house around the bay then they could wake their mom and dad to get their Christmas morning started. If not, back to bed! They looked and were lucky, there were a few lights in houses around the bay already, because many houses had children, who were Madison and Arthur's friends living in them. It was such an exciting time. They ran up the stairs to wake their mom and dad. "How could anybody sleep on Christmas morning," thought Madison? Their parent got dressed and came down stairs while Arthur and Madison settled in a big chair to receive their gifts. As was tradition, they both knew mom or dad would call out the name on the gift one at a time. Mom wanted to cook their traditional Christmas morning breakfast of homemade toast, juice, bacon and eggs, but they were too excited to wait for that, they just wanted to get their gifts immediately like all kids, on Christmas morning. Fortunately, today their mom and dad went directly to the Christmas tree. The traditions continued with the name of the person receiving the gift and who it was from, read out one at a time, until all gifts were removed from under the tree.

Arthur was hoping to get some fishing gear this year because, if he did, he knew that meant he would definitely be going fishing with his father the next spring or summer.

Their mother called out the names on presents as Arthur and his sister unwrapped them for a look. Their dad wrote down who gave the present and what the present was. This was really great for later to remember who gave them what present, so they could say thank you properly to all their friends and relatives. As the number of presents under the tree dwindled, Arthur began to get concerned, he had not received any fishing gear yet. Soon all the presents were open and a pile of gift wrapping paper lay scattered about the floor.

Although he was very happy with his presents there was a hint of disappointment in his voice because he had not received the most important thing he wanted, fishing gear. His mother sensed there was something wrong. His mother asked him if everything was okay. Arthur replied, 'Yes mom,' not wanting to complain about his many presents. It was at that moment his father removed something from behind the tree. "I wonder who this is for?" he said as he revealed the best looking fishing rod Arthur had ever seen. Byron read the tag out loud "To Byron from Jack". Arthur felt disappointment in his heart and stomach and he began to cry. As tears flowed down his cheek, all of a sudden he heard his father say, "I am only joking Arthur, it reads; to Arthur from Santa Clause". His tears of disappointment turned to tears of joy. It was the happiest day of his life. Arthur noticed a white envelope attached to the fishing rod. The name on the envelope read; "To Arthur." He had not noticed it behind the tree because it was well hidden to be revealed as a last minute surprise by his father who knew how desperately Arthur wanted fishing equipment.

The gifts opened and surprises complete, Agnes and Byron went into the kitchen to make a family breakfast. The house was soon filled with the smell of bacon and eggs cooking on the wood and oil stove in the kitchen. The children waited, reviewed their presents and played with any gifts they could. Arthur had received a couple of video games he so wanted to try out but his mom said, "not until after breakfast because it is important to eat together as a family on Christmas Day and give thanks for all the gifts received. Santa Claus and God had been very generous this year."

After a having the breakfast prepared by mom and dad, their parents went back to bed for more sleep while the children settled in to enjoy their presents and Christmas morning. At 10 A.M. their parents came down stairs, to get ready for another Christmas tradition; Christmas Catholic Mass. Agnes would stay home to cook the meal today while Byron took the children to mass.

Arthur and Madison were not interested in going to Catholic Mass or any church on Christmas morning but it was a requirement of their mother. It was the tradition she grew up with. Mass on special days and Saturday evening or Sunday mornings every week. It was good to teach them about God and to instill some morals their mom always said. Attending Mass together was an important part of family life.

After Catholic mass on Christmas day, Byron took them to the cemetery to visit their mother's parents grave, their Nan and Papa. The cemetery was just a few minutes' walk from the church parking lot. Arthur and his sister did not understand why they did this. As they mature into adults, that memory would take on more significance, especially when they heard stories about their grandparents from their parents and relatives.

Arthur was very happy today because he had added another very important item of fishing gear to his gear collection. Soon Arthur would own all the fishing gear he would need for his long dreamed about fishing trip with his dad to Red Harbour Fall's ponds.

Byron took Arthur and Madison to mass while their mom prepared the traditional Newfoundland home cooked meal, a Christmas Jiggs Dinner. Jiggs dinner consisted of a stuffed turkey, slow roasted in the oven for hours (starting about 8 A.M), salt beef that had been soaked in water overnight then placed in the large pot referred to as a boiler to start the meal cooking preparation. The remainder required items were all added to a pot one at a time to ensure all was cooked and ready to eat precisely at the same time. This was the standard meal in Newfoundland homes for special occasions and Sunday dinners, usually served at about 12 noon. On Christmas day, dinner was normally 1:00 P.M., to give more time for preparation and the Christmas church service.

Byron and the children arrived home from church just as Agnes was removing the stuffed and ready to eat Turkey from the oven. 'Dinner sure smells great,' said Byron, as he entered the kitchen, "let me give you a hand with that honey," he said. "Thanks, you can carve it," said Agnes. Agnes yelled to her children, "You two can go play with your gifts, until your father and I finish preparing dinner, and ensure you wash up before dinner," Arthur and Madison went to retrieve a favored gift from under the Christmas tree. Arthur selected a Nintendo game, Zelda. Madison asked if she could also play and Arthur agreed, happy to have his sister play along with him.

At dinner mom, Agnes asked, "Okay children, what did the priest talk about today in mass?" Madison chimed in, "Same as every Christmas mom, the story of the Nativity, the birth of the baby Jesus. Mom was impressed the Madison remembered. 'Well, she said without the birth of Jesus there would not be a Christmas celebration. The birth of Jesus is why we celebrate Christmas. "She went on to say, "The three wise men were led by the star of Bethlehem to the place where Jesus was born and they brought gifts for him, so that is why we give and receive gifts at Christmas." " I know said Arthur that's why Christmas is special, he went on with a question, "I wonder why we keep celebrating Jesus birthday even though he is not around anymore. "Good question Arthur, said Byron. There was silence as Byron thought for a moment than went on to say "Arthur, Jesus was God's gift to the world, It's my understanding, Jesus most likely was not actually born this time of year." Byron continued with his answer, Christmas was not always a religious holiday it was initiated by Christianity to try to curb people celebrating pagan festivals at that time of year, therefore his actual birthday probably was not on this day but the important thing is we celebrate it." Byron went on to say, "Families also celebrate because it is an extended holiday and gives them a chance to get together with all family and friends and it also marks the end of another year." Agnes stated, "It's good to celebrate a positive happening in a world, where bad things happen and it's a great chance to enjoy our extended families, like having a big house party and feast like we do on Boxing Day night" when our family and friends come to share the celebration. Agnes continued, "We get a chance catch up with each other's life, have a few laughs and to play and listen to music and dance." "Okay let's say grace to give thanks now," said Byron, "Let's get eating before the food gets cold."

As the family enjoyed their tasty Christmas dinner made up of Stuffed Roasted Turkey, salt beef, Carrots, Parsnips, Turnip, Cabbage, potatoes, pea's pudding and gravy, Agnes had prepared, few words were spoken. 'This meal is so good, you have out done yourself today mom," said Byron. The children nodded their head in agreement.

As dinner was finishing, Byron asked Agnes if she was interested in doing some mummering later after dark. "I would love to," stated Agnes.

Disguising one's self as Mummers is a long standing Christmas tradition in Newfoundland when people dress up in homemade costumes to hide their identity and walk house to house knocking on local house doors, asking in a disguised voice, "Are any mummers allowed in." Usually the mummers are invited in to alcohol drinks and Christmas fruit cake served by the hosts. In many cases drinks and food are followed by some great Irish Newfoundland dance music. The mummers always invited their host to dance, when the host did not want to dance which was not often the case, the mummers danced with each other as their host laughed, clapped their hands and cheered them on. Usually all had a good time before moving on to another house repeating the same tradition over and over again until the mummers were too drunk or too tired to continue. After a great night of celebrating the mummers returned home tired and happy from their night of merry making.

12

Carving

January started with a fierce winter storm that closed roads and businesses The important happening for Arthur and Madison was, school was closed. All kids love a storm day, creating a school holiday. Due to the weather, mom and dad were not working today either, so all would be inside today until shoveling snow was necessary, after the snow stopped falling. As the family ate a hot breakfast prepared by Dad they could see out the big kitchen window near the table. The window towards the ocean cove was referred to as a bay window because it was a large glass window facing the ocean. The wind blowing onto the window was so strong it caused the glass to buckle, which worried Byron. He found an old hockey stick and cut the handle to a length creating a brace for the window in an X pattern to prevent the strong wind from breaking it. The wind blew strong, and the sea surf pounded the shore line as icy snow pounded against the window. Occasionally the house would shake from a strong gust of wind.

Their house stood very near the shoreline of the harbour. It was common to be able to step from their patio and take a few steps on a short path to the ocean beach behind their house. Today their view of the ocean was somewhat obscured by the wind and driving snow that was howling up the bay. Although Arthur was a little concerned about the storm his dad and mom were very calm about it all. Arthur's father said "it is important to stay calm in a storm to avoid doing anything stupid."

All the family were required to sit at the table together for meals. Today breakfast was no different, as they all sat down to eat. Video games of Nintendo, TV or phone calls, were not permitted during meal times. The family always said grace, gave thanks to God, and being Catholic blessed themselves before a meal and talked about things going on in their lives. During breakfast Agnes said, "Today is a good day to catch up on your school work. Who has unfinished homework?" That was the last question Arthur and Madison wanted to hear on a storm day at home. That thought was disappointing. They just wanted to go outside into the storm and go sledding on the hill near the house. Their mom and dad said "maybe later when the storm starts to quiet a little." Dad said, "I am sure later I will need some help shoveling the driveway." Mom and dad removed the dishes from the table after breakfast and directed the children to wash, dry and put them into the cupboards. Their parents always jokingly said," we do not need an automatic dish washer we already have two."

Arthur and his sister found their book bags exactly where they last left them, hanging on the stairway banister railing post leading to the second floor. The stairway and railings were the original staircase built in the house when it was constructed about a 100 years ago. The wear over the years was still visible on the uncovered staircase steps and railings. The many markings were left intentionally by the children's parents during renovations of the old house. On the railing, still visible were pocket knife cuts and initials of first loves carved into the railings and posts. Those carvings were completed by Arthur and

Madison's aunts and uncles, their mother and her siblings, who all grew up in the house. The stairway was kind of a timeline history. A timeline history of their grandparents.

This railings, their mom said, was the same railings their grandmother used to lean on to get up and down stairs while she was carrying all of her children including her. Some markings appeared to have been carved using the sharp end of a divider from a grade school geometry set. Ironically, the carvings in the wood railing may have taken place on a school storm day after their aunts and uncles were sent upstairs to catch up on school work by Madison and Arthur's grandparents.

Today Arthur thought, maybe he would carve his initials on this timeline to leave his mark on the old house. To achieve his goal he would need a pocket knife. He did not own a geometry set yet, but he knew just where to find a pocket knife, the one his father owned. Arthur, hatched a plan because he thought, if he asked for a pocket knife his father's answer would be, "not today my son you will cut yourself but when you get older I will buy you a knife".

Arthur went to his parents' bedroom and looked directly in the place he knew his father kept the knife. The boy let out a breath and said, "Wow." There it was, a beautiful red Swiss Army pocket knife. It was much more than a knife. This knife included a can opener, a bottle opener, scissors, pliers, tweezers, and tooth pick and three different size cutting blades. A fancy knife it was and the young boy was impressed by its beauty and all the many options included in it. This was the type of knife he wanted to own one day. A knife like this would be great to use on his much dreamed about fishing trips with his dad. Arthur felt a pain of guilt as he removed the knife from its hiding place without asking his father permission, but continued anyway. He had heard his father occasionally say, "Sometimes it may be better to ask for forgiveness than permission." "This could be that type of occasion" he thought. Arthur creeped back to the stairs with the knife in hand.

The knife blades were difficult to open. Just as he was successful in opening the knife, the door at the bottom of the stairs opened and with that Arthur closed the knife and rushed back to his parents' bedroom to replace the knife. He realized it was his mother that was coming up the stairs. As his mother entered the bedroom Agnes asked Arthur, "What are you doing here?" The startled Arthur stated "well I was hoping to borrow dad's knife to carve my initials into the stairway railing just like my aunts and uncles did long ago." His mother did not seem surprised at that thought, she just said "I was wondering when this day would come, it appears it's here."

Then Mom said "It is stormy out today so let's you and I get the knife and I will ask your father to help you with your carving." Arthur's heart skipped a beat at that thought and said "really mom?!" "Yes," said his mother, as she walked across the room and fished the pocket knife from its hiding place, where Byron had placed it, and handed it to him. "You will have to be careful," she said, 'I'll let your father know". "Okay great," he said with excitement as he headed toward the stairs. Then Mom said, "Do not do anything until your father and I are ready, okay?" Arthur, with the knife in hand, sat on the stair at the top of the staircase to wait for his mom and dad.

As he waited he could hear his parents talking and he thought he heard the word "no" from his father. With that word, his heart sank a little, but then the door opened and both his parents were standing at the bottom of the stairs, with a big smile, looking up at him. "I hear you want to carve your initials into the stair railings," his father said. "Yes please," said Arthur. Byron replied, "Okay give me the knife my son." Arthur handed the knife to his dad. His father said, "Let me show you how to use this knife to carve your initials." As he opened one of the blades, the smallest blade, he said, "This one will be the easiest for you to do your work. You will have to do it slowly and carefully to avoid cutting yourself, okay?" He handed the knife back to Arthur who was very pleased to have it. Mom said, "You have to find a place not previously used, not an easy task on this banister rail." Together they found a suitable place to start carving. Arthur slowly began cutting into the railing using shallow cuts and digging out the bits of wood as his dad talked him through it. He carved his initials, A.S.C. into the wood. The carving took the young boy about an hour or more under his father's guidance.

Just as Arthur was about to finish the carving, his little sister Madison came onto the stairs from the family room. She promptly asked, "Can I carve my name too"? Dad said to her "I do not think you can do this yet young lady without cutting yourself, so you will have to wait until you get older and bigger like your brother. Then you can carve into the railing the like Arthur has." That comment by dad made Arthur feel good knowing he had done something his sister was not big and old enough to do. Madison asked, "How soon will that be dad?" "Well", said Byron "at the rate you are growing that will be in about two years". His sister was not happy with that answer, but let it go for now. Then dad said to her "you go down stairs and get the monopoly board ready. We can play a game after we finish here." Madison hung her head, disappointed, but said "Okay" as she headed down stairs to find the board game to set it up on the kitchen table.

As Arthur finished the carving of initials he stepped back and looked with pride of what he had done. Arthur now had joined the memories of his aunts and uncles, adding his mark to the railings timeline. Byron then patted Arthur on the head and said "great job my son". Arthur was very pleased with his work. He knew he had added his own mark to this old house that would be visible for many years, at least as long as the old house would be left standing.

The storm had passed by early-afternoon and the family's life soon turned to shoveling snow, and activities of cleaning up after a winter storm. The driveway to the house was about fifteen meters long with a steep slope to the street. Dad, mom, Arthur and Madison all had their own shovels. The whole family worked together to clear the snow.

During the snow removal the family played a little tossing snow at each other and chasing around with a snow filled mitt to toss snow down somebody's neck just for laughs. After all the work and fun it was time to relax and get warm with a drink of hot chocolate.

Another successful family snow day.

13

Birthday

As winter passed, Arthur spent a little of each day dreaming. Occasionally he got in trouble at school due to his day dreaming of his anticipated fishing trip, not always listening to his teacher.

Soon it was March and Arthur's birthday was a few days away. He was thinking about his birthday, hoping and wondering about the presents he would get this year.

The day before his birthday Arthur came home from school and entered the house to the smell of cake that was baking. He had asked many of his friends at school along with his closest friends Jimmy and Billy, to his house for a birthday party his parents had planned for him tomorrow. Most of his friends had accepted the birthday invitation. It was not going to be a large number. As Arthur entered the house his mother asked' "So, how many are coming for your birthday party tomorrow"? "Eight," he answered. "That will be enough," his mother replied.

Arthur went to bed that night thinking about his birthday party and the presents he wished for. As he drifted off to sleep his thoughts were about getting the remainder of the fishing gear he would need to go fishing with his father. He hoped he would get his most wanted items for his birthday. Arthur had not heard or saw anything to indicate what his presents were going to be. His thoughts were of the gear he wanted, a fishing tackle box filled with bobbers, different kinds of fishing hooks, including swivels and sinkers, and a special container to carry worms for bait. Then, oh then, he drifted off to sleep.

The next morning, his birthday, Arthur woke up earlier than usual, in a good mood and to birthday wishes from his sister and parents as they prepared a special breakfast for him. A breakfast made up of his favorite, blueberry waffles with maple syrup, and whipped cream. So good! As they went off to school Arthur was filled with anticipation of his birthday party. Super was going to be early because his friends were planning to arrive immediately after school was out for the day.

Arthur hurried home after school with his sister Madison by the hand. During the school year, it was his responsibility to ensure his sister got home safe from school. Sometimes he just wanted to go play with his friends but he loved his sister so much and wanted to ensure she was always home safely, besides if he did not get his sister home safe right after school he would catch it from his parents. He noticed his sister was growing and was making friends at school and soon would not need him to ensure she was home safely.

Today as they got home, his parents were outside waiting for them. "Happy birthday" they said as they gave them both a big hug and kiss on the cheek. They all went inside to wait for his friends to arrive. As they walked inside Arthur noticed a table in the family room his mother had prepared for his friends to lay any gifts on. The house smelled like mom had been baking all day. A smell he would always remember as he grew older.

He noticed cupcakes decorated with chocolate icing and multicolored candy sprinkles sitting on a tray on the counter in the pantry. As he walked by them, "Yummy," he said out loud. His mom smiled at the comment and said "a special treat for you on your birthday my son. I also have a special birthday cake that you will see when all your friends are here, but not until you all finish eating." That thought made Arthur very happy; he knew his mother was a good baker and could make great cakes of all kinds and shapes. He really was looking forward to this special birthday cake mom had made for him.

Arthur went upstairs to change into his jeans and a sweater his mom had laid out on his bed for him. After changing his clothes, fixing his hair and washing his hands, he came back down stairs to greet his friends who were already arriving. Two of his best friends Billy and Jimmy had arrived first. Not long after, the rest of his friends arrived. All of them had brought a wrapped present or a card in an envelope with his name on it. Agnes (mom) told all his friends to lay the presents on the table she had prepared. "Arthur will open his presents after you all finish eating" she said.

Although it was a little chilly out, they all went outside to play baseball in the meadow, close to Arthur's family home. Before going outside the kids all got a cupcake that mom was giving out. She said "just a little something to help tide you hungry boys over until supper". Byron organized the ball game outside by choosing Arthur and his best friend Billy for team captions to pick their teams, flipping a coin for choice to pick first, alternating between them choosing one at a time. There was one problem, Arthur's little sister also wanted to play. The boy's thought she really was too little to play. Byron said Madison could play also, but only in the outfield for both teams. That idea made her very happy, she was included! She ran into the meadow to play. The game got underway with dad being the umpire and catching for both teams.

Soon mom was calling everybody inside to eat the meal of hamburgers, hot dogs, and potato salad. Chips and fruit were also available, and all the condiments. Arthur and his friends' favorite foods.

Arthur was in for a surprise today: a special birthday cake and something special his parents had not yet revealed. As supper was finishing, Arthur parents brought out the General Lee birthday cake. A cake decorated as a car, with the same colors as seen on Arthur's favorite TV program, The Dukes of Hazzard. The famous (to Arthur) car driven by Bowe and Luke Duke.

With candles now burning, Arthur's friends, led by Arthur's mom and dad, sang happy birthday. Arthur thought his mom had done a great job making and decorating the cake. He was very pleased. Agnes served out generous portions of birthday cake and ice cream to all. As the last scraps of cake was eaten, Arthur waved his arm and said, "Come on boys follow me," as he walked into the family room to open presents.

All of Arthur's friends followed him into the living room as Agnes played happy birthday on the piano. He opened his gifts one at a time, reading the name of the gift giver before opening it. There were the usual cards with money, but close friends gave gift wrapped presents, a Nintendo video game and another board game. As the number of presents dwindled his heart sank a little as he realized he did not have a present from his mom and dad or sister.

As he was feeling a little sorry for himself, his family, Byron, Agnes and Madison appeared with a big box wrapped in bright birthday paper and began singing happy birthday. Arthur and his friends was excited to get the present opened. He ripped the ribbon, paper and bows from the box. As he looked inside, his heart felt very happy. He noticed it was full of the fishing gear he would need to go fishing with his father. He unloaded the box onto the floor to show his friends. There was a Mitchell reel for his Mitchell fishing rod, plus many types of fishing hooks, lures, bobbers, sinker weights, and a tackle box, a bag to hang over his shoulders to carry gear, a pair of long rubber boots and a pair of gloves. Now he had everything he needed to go fishing with his father. Arthur was so excited and immediately was looking forward to school finishing for the year in June, just a few months away because he knew now it was a sure thing he was going fishing this summer.

14

Sibling Secrets

That night Arthur went to bed very happy, as he drifted off to sleep he had visions of catching a big fish. He was already planning the fishing trip because now he owned the fishing equipment he needed. Arthur knew his father was definitely planning to take him to Red Harbour Falls Ponds when school was out for summer.

The next morning Arthur had a big smile on his face as he headed to school with his little sister by the hand. He told his sister about the fishing trip he was planning. Sticking out his chest a little. Arthur said, "I am going because I am the oldest and biggest".

They were soon at the point where he dropped his sister at her school. Madison was almost in tears as she ran to play with her little friends. She looked back at her brother and said, "I want to go fishing with you and dad also". "I will ask dad later," she said. "Oh no'" said Arthur, "if you do that, dad could get upset at me and decide not to take me at all". "I will not take you anywhere with me again if you do that," he said. Then he said "if you do not say anything I will try to get dad to take you and I somewhere fishing together" not so far away. Madison agreed to that and ran off.

Arthur was a little worried as he walked alone, to his own school. Arthur knew his little sister usually did not keep secrets very well. He felt sorry for even talking about the fishing trip with her. That same afternoon as they walked home from school, Madison did not mention the fishing trip. That made him happy, hoping his sister had forgotten the conversation they had earlier in the day.

When Arthur and Madison arrived home the house was empty which was odd because usually mom or dad were home. As Arthur and his sister entered the house their noses caught the smell of home baking. Almost together they both said mmm fresh baked cookies. Sure enough there were fresh chocolate chip cookies on the counter top. "Let's have Milk and cookies," said Madison as she went to the refrigerator to get the milk. "Good idea", said Arthur as he helped his sister get glasses and pour the milk. Soon both of them were sitting at the table having a great after school snack.

Just as they were finishing eating they heard a car in the driveway. It was mom. "I was hoping to get home before you two got home," she said. "No harm done, you are doing okay taking care of yourselves", and I am proud of you," she said. "I was so worried about not being here when you got home, I was rushing", but I see there was no need to rush at all." Both children grew a little taller hearing the compliments from their mother.

15

Schools Out

June finally arrived and the last day of school for Arthur. Finally! Arthur could barely wait to see the last minute of that school day and school year. He felt really excited as he walked home knowing in his heart Dad would soon be taking him on the fishing trip he had been dreaming about for a long time. Arthur arrived home from his last day of school and noticed his father was not home from work yet. He could barely wait until Byron got home. Arthur was excitedly hoping his father was going to discuss a fishing trip plan during supper that evening. Arthur often checked the time showing on the electric clock hanging on the wall in the kitchen, time was so slow, he thought. Arthur noted the clock showed 5 P.M. Soon his father would be home. At 6 P.M. he became worried because his father had not yet arrived home.

The phone rang, his mother answered, it was Byron saying he had to work late, but hoped to be home before the kids went to bed. Arthur felt a pain of disappointment when he realized he would have to wait to talk to his father. Arthur wanted this fishing trip so badly and now school was out for summer. The thoughts in his brain were loud and clear. Dad will be planning a fishing trip with him soon for sure. That evening the hours passed very slowly as he kept checking the clock. He tried to keep busy, helping mom wash the dinner dishes and playing video games, but no matter how hard he tried he could not get his mind away from that fishing trip.

Finally it was 9 P.M and he heard his dad arrive in the driveway. Arthur ran out to welcome his dad home, hoping he would want to discuss that fishing trip to Red Harbour Falls Ponds. As Byron got out of the car he noticed Arthur standing by the side of the driveway. "Hello my son, how was your day?" "Well, I finished school today," Arthur said. "So I heard, let's go inside and talk while I eat supper," Byron said. Once inside Byron went upstairs to shower and change while Arthur waited impatiently at the table in the kitchen. As Byron was going upstairs he heard his wife say, "A little boy seems to want to talk to his dad about something important, please listen to what he has to say. Then Arthur heard dad say, "I bet I know exactly what it is."

After taking a shower and getting a change of cloth, Byron came back down stairs. As Byron entered the kitchen he noticed Arthur sitting at the table. "So I hear you may want to talk to me." "What is it, my son?" Arthur was a little apprehensive and nervous because he was worried about the answer his dad would give him, maybe he had changed his mind about taking him fishing. "Well dad", Arthur said, "Now that school is out for the summer, I was wondering if you were still going to take me fishing to the Red Harbour Falls Ponds as you promised last summer." Then Arthur heard what he had been hoping for since last he could remember. Byron said, "Of course my son, I was talking to Jack about that just today, I called him from work." Our plan is to take you fishing with us this weekend on Saturday if the weather is okay. At that moment Arthur felt the excitement shiver through his body. Okay! Great, he said "thanks dad, I love you so much". "I love you to my son" Byron said as he reached for Arthur and placed his arms around him for a big hug. Arthur then ran outside. He ran to the top of the hill near their house. Arthur arrived at the top of the hill and turned east toward his friend Billy's house.

Then with arms raised into the air he yelled as loud as he possibly could, "I am going to Red Harbour Falls Pond fishing with my dad". Yaaaaaaaaaa! The yell was followed by a much quieter calmer voice with an out loud prayer, "Thanks God, "Arthur said in an excited tone of voice. The yelling seemed to quiet his excitement and made the fishing trip real. Arthur felt so good. tonight he will sleep well.

Arthur was very happy when he came back inside. He looked at his dad and said, 'I will check my fishing gear tomorrow morning right after breakfast. "Arthur, it's time for bed," his mom said. Agnes went upstairs to tuck Arthur into bed and ensure he said his bedtime prayers. After getting Arthur into bed, Agnes came back down stairs, she had a look of pride on her face as she sat down next to her husband and leaned over to give him a hug and kiss.

Agnes said, "You are a great dad, you have made our son so happy he will not sleep a minute before Saturday, he has been thinking about this day for such a long time." "God bless him." "So have I my love, I think this will be the best fishing trip ever "Byron said. His voice lowered as it cracked with emotion. "I will look in on him when I go up to bed." "You know you will have to," said Agnes.

16

Jack

Saturday morning came, Arthur and Byron were up at 6 A.M. Jack would be here to pick them up at 7:30 A.M. in his SUV Jeep. Arthur was so excited he hardly slept at all and hoped he was not too tired for the walk to Red Harbour Falls. Byron made a very light breakfast for them because he was planning to cook a big breakfast when they arrived at the pond. Today was a warm sunny day with only a slight warm breeze from the south. A great day for fishing.

At about 7:25 A.M. Jack arrived in the driveway. Just as they were about to go outside, Agnes arrived in the kitchen. She said," I just came down stairs to give my two men a hug and kiss goodbye." She seemed so very proud and pleased with Arthur this morning giving him an extra big hug and kiss as he rushed out the door to meet Jack who was waiting for them. Byron soon joined them. As Byron was closing the SUV doors Arthur heard his mom say, "I love you both, enjoy the fishing". "We will" they both yelled back

When all three were comfortable in the SUV with seat belts on, Jack started to joke with Arthur. "Where do you think you are going this morning Arthur," he asked? "Going fishing with you and dad," said Arthur proudly. "Oh," said Jack. "Well, I got news for you, we are only going to Tim Hortons for a coffee and breakfast, and maybe you can walk home from there." Both dad and Jack started to laugh. "Sorry buddy," Byron said. Arthur knew Jack well and knew he was a jokester. Arthur said with a chuckle, "well when you get out of the truck I will drive dad and I, we already have the fishing gear in the jeep. "To that Jack said "I will call the cops and tell them you stole my jeep, then you and your father will be in jail, what do you think of that young fellow?" As the SUV neared the Tim Horton turn off, Jack made the turn and did not stop but drove right through to order at the drive through. He ordered a coffee for him and Byron then looked at Arthur and said "I would order you one young fellow but coffee shrinks your penis and yours is already small enough. "Everybody laughed, including Arthur. Although he felt a little embarrassed. Arthur knew it was just Jack being Jack.

Soon the trio were on the highway and headed toward Red Harbour. As they drove Byron and Jack drank their coffee and laughed and joked about the upcoming golf season.

During the summer, Byron and Jack often drove to Terra Nova National Park to play golf for a few days. There was not a golf course in their area just yet, although one would be built in later years.

After about half an hour driving Arthur noticed Jack had slowed down and turned on his signal light to make a left turn just before the highway bridge crossing the Red Harbour River. As they turned left onto an old gravel dirt road. Arthur thought, " this must be the place to park to start the walk to Red Harbour Falls."

After a couple minutes of driving slowly Jack stopped the SUV just in front of what was an old concrete bridge over a small river. "This old bridge may not be safe to drive over," said Jack, "We have to go take a look." They all got out of the truck to look. This old concrete bridge that had not been in use for many years. The old bridge was worse for wear and had lots of over growth at each end. As they walked out on the bridge over the river, a tributary of the bigger Red Harbour River, Arthur noticed this bridge was not in good shape. There was at least a three meter drop to the river below. The bridge was not completely bridged over; it had a few small holes in its concrete deck and did not look safe to Arthur but Jack and Byron said it looked fine for today and headed back to the SUV.

Jack carefully drove his SUV over the old bridge. After crossing the bridge they continued on the old dirt road. This road was not much more than a path now overgrown on each side with grass and Alders bushes. There were tree branches protruding out into the road from both sides. Arthur also noted the old road had many loose stones and many potholes. Jack jokingly said "I better be careful I don't want to miss any of those pot holes or get lost in one."

Arthur felt his belly flutter with excitement and a little nervousness all at once, he was finally here. The place he had only dreamed about. The old road was a short distance from the river. The river that was flowing from the Red Harbour Falls pond where Arthur was headed today. Arthur noticed from the SUV back seat side window there was a gentle slope down toward the river located about two hundred meters from the road side. "Arthur, that is the Red Harbour River my boy," stated Jack. From his vantage point, Arthur noticed the land sloped toward the river was covered with short brush and dotted with a few short trees that appeared to be strategically put in place by Mother Nature to block his full view of the river. As the SUV slowed down Arthur could also see a slightly worn footpath leading possibly to the river bank. He followed the path with his eyes until it disappeared from sight into the short bushes that were growing along the river bank. His view also revealed the other side of the river had a thick growth of spruce and evergreen trees.

The SUV slowed more as Jack scanned the roadside for a place to pull over to the side of the old road to park. Jack soon was parked, "Let's get going," he said. Okay Byron said "let's get our gear and get started up river to the falls." Arthur felt so excited he thought he may urinate in his pants in the SUV if he did not get out quickly.

Jack and Byron headed to the rear of the SUV to retrieve the fishing gear and food. Arthur walked to the front area and found a tree to stand behind to tinkle. As soon as he was finished he went to help get the gear out of the SUV.

The group removed their street foot wear to pull on their rubber hip waders that would be needed to travel up river and also be required for fishing at the pond. Arthur was proud of his new pair of waders his father had purchased for him. Jack said, "Arthur buddy, I think walking and carrying yourself is enough for you to handle today."

Jack and Byron loaded their pack sacks filled with the food and fishing gear onto their backs. Byron looked at Arthur and then asked, "Would you like to carry your own fishing rod buddy"? "Yes, I will," said Arthur with a big grin showing much pride in himself.

Jack secured his SUV, before all three of them started down the path toward the river with Jack in the lead. Arthur followed second and Byron stayed back to the rear. Byron was behind Arthur, because of his concern for his son. Byron knew the trip was not going to be an easy one for Arthur. Byron also knew his son needed to know he could do this and it would boost his confidence.

Just as the group reached the trees lining the river's bank Jack stopped suddenly. He dropped back behind Byron and as Arthur passed he took Arthur's fishing rod from his hand and said," I will take that through the trees so you will not get tangled up in the branches". "Great idea," Byron stated." "Follow me boys," Byron said, as he disappeared into the trees, with Arthur close on his heels. Arthur and his dad broke through to the trees lining the river bank very quickly but where was Jack. Suddenly Byron and Arthur heard a big yell and a curse coming from a few meters away. It was Jack.

"You okay" Bryon yelled," "I am fine" yelled Jack, 'but I cannot say the same for my backpack." "I guess I will have to show you how it's done," Byron said jokingly." Just then Jack came onto the river bank to join Byron and Arthur. 'You show me," said Jack. Jack looked at Arthur and winked, "we will see who shows who when we get to the pond." Then Byron said to Jack, "I forgot more about fishing than you have ever known buddy". Arthur had a laugh at how his dad and Jack were joking with each other. Arthur knew they were great buddies just having a little fun.

Today was a beautiful sunny morning, hardly a cloud in the sky. There was a complete silence except from the moving about and breathing from human activity. They were alone in the world it seemed. "Beautiful! Just beautiful!" Jack explained as he took a deep breath and slowly exhaled. "It is that my friend, enough to make a grown man cry," said Byron. Take a look Arthur and drink this in my son, "Byron said," You will never forget this day and neither will I." The three fishermen stood still on the bank of the river, nobody was moving or talking. The only other sounds that could be heard was the river water rushing by.

The sun was gleaming through the tops of the trees on the other side of the river. Shining through its rays like fingers gently brushing their faces with a loving touch as if to say I will give you a great day today, the best of me. The fisherman saw and felt the sun's fingers as it reached out its gentle touch with promises of a great day ahead.

Arthur noted as he stood silently, the only sound he could hear was a light rustle of the trees and the river. As he looked around, he marveled at how fast the river current was moving along. His eyes followed the current down river. He noticed the large boulders in the water that the river water swished around making ripples and babbling sounds as it flowed around them, until it disappeared out of sight around a bend about a hundred meters down river. As he listened closely, the babbling of the water reminded him of a baby's laugh.

The river bank had some low bushes and tall grass that was taller than Arthur. Byron looked at his son and said," you did a great job getting down here my boy," but along the river will not be an easy walk for a while and will get harder in some places as we travel up river" Arthur did not like the idea of the walk to the Falls getting harder because he wanted to do this without help. He wanted to prove to dad and Jack he was growing into a strong and capable young man.

"We have to get going," Jack said, as he turned and started up the river with Arthur and Byron following. Byron was intentionally walking slower than he and Jack normally walked. Byron realized his son was just a young boy and would not keep up if the hike was at their normal pace. He also knew it was important to build the confidence of his young son, to know he could keep up with them.

The grass became shorter as they came to a place in the river where brush and trees blocked their way. A few tree branches over hung the river. This area required them to wade out into the river to get past. As Arthur walked out into the river a few feet he was having difficulty getting through just as he heard Jack say," Arthur, my boy you can do this, I am behind you, take your time." Arthur noted his new hip waders were barely high enough to walk through the water without the river water filling his boots. Arthur thought," I am happy my feet are staying dry because water in my boots would make my walking more difficult than it already is".

The group were soon free of the difficult area and back onto the river bank path. Looking back over his shoulder at his son Byron said, "Great job buddy." Then Arthur heard Jack say "I think we should have a little rest', as he found a boulder on the river bank to sit on. "Great idea," said Byron but just for a few minutes." Arthur was happy to sit for a while because he was feeling a little tired and overwhelmed but was not wanting to complain. Arthur felt the warm sun on his face and enjoyed how it felt. Arthur sat and then noticed the other side of the river had a steep bank with a gravel and rocky shore line along the river edge. He saw an eagle flying just above the tree line on the other side and marveled at its wingspan. The eagle was very visible against the backdrop of green trees and blue sky. "Do you see that eagle over there?" his father asked. "Yes" said Arthur as he watched in awe of the flight of the big bird, as it glided along. The eagle gently flapped its wings. Arthur had seen eagles many times but this seemed different as if it was suspended in air. He could hear its wing swoosh, swoosh, breaking the silence. 'Wow, what an awesome view," he thought, as he drank it in.

17

The Long Walk

Byron, Arthur, and Jack, again headed up the river feeling a little rested. As they walked they could hear the river babbling as it flowed and noticed as the river in its hurried rush down river created undercurrents.

The group soon came to another place in the river where the brush and trees along the River Bank covered the bank right up to the river's edge. This area would require a new approach by making them enter the river water to walk around the tree branches that were overhanging the river, or try to find a path around it, if the river was too deep here. Jack entered the river first. Byron said to Arthur, "you go ahead of me, follow Jack and I will keep an eye on you while you're out in the river". Arthur entered the river, his legs unsteady in the rushing Water. He found himself struggling to push the tree branches back to allow himself access to walk by, without getting water into his Waders. Just as a branch was pushing him backwards into the river he felt his father's strong arms, under his armpits, scooping him up to carry him forward. "I have you" his dad said, "We got this". Arthur was happy his father had decided to lift him up to carry him past the tree branches and the deeper River water. Jack had already reached the riverbank past the trees and was sitting waiting when Byron and Arthur arrived. "What was the matter with you, Arthur, your legs are too short" Jack said with a laugh? Byron said "no he just needed a little help is all, people need a little help sometimes, same as Arthur did."

How far have we walked Arthur asked? "We are about three km in and we have at least one more km to go" Byron answered. Arthur looked up to see the river branched into two tributaries just ahead. This is the place your uncle got us lost a few years ago, and I will not make that mistake today, laughed Byron. Do you remember that story my son? You can point us the way today." That worried Arthur because he did not know the correct direction to go. "I am sure, dad knows which directions to go," he thought. To the left stated Arthur? "That is correct young fellow," said Jack. Arthur felt very proud of himself. He had listened and learned well from the stories told by his uncles at his house.

This area of the river produced a lot of water and a lot of current because two river branches were joined into one, to make a much larger River. At this location most of he river had a gravel shore making it easy to walk. In one area the riverbank was especially high, and hard to navigate around. This high spot was at the location the river changed direction. This point where the Rivers two branches came together and changed direction, the river's current had torn trees and earth from the riverbank causing the river to flow erratically and creating a big current and rough water where the river narrowed to continue downstream. Arthur was really impressed with the river. "It's like dad said,' he said out loud to himself." Byron said, "There is a lot of water because of the winter snow melt and the amount of rain that falls in our Newfoundland spring."

"No rain today though, just beautiful sunshine, a clear blue sky and just a slight warm breeze from the South." Jack said," The waterfalls and ponds are this way boy's". "We have to go this way boy's to the falls like Arthur said," he yelled, his voice barely heard over the sound of the rushing water. As he made the left turn to continue onto the bank of the river branch, Jack would lead them to the falls and ponds today. Arthur felt the pings of excitement in his belly and chest as they headed up the river.

"This should be the final stage of walking toward the falls and the fishing ponds," Arthur thought. He was getting more excited with every step. "We will be there soon my son," Byron said. "You are doing a great job of walking the river Arthur," Those words made Arthur feel really proud of himself because he knew his Dad and Jack were concerned about taking him along. Byron and Jack had made this walk many times and knew it could be a long and difficult walk to the falls and climb up to the ponds above for a young boy such as Arthur.

Byron looked at Jack and said, "He is doing much better than I thought." "He is doing great for a little fellow with short legs like you," Jack said with a laugh. "We cannot all be giants like you Jack," Byron said with a chuckle." Then Byron said to Jack. "The only reason you are here is because the missus kicked you out of bed to get rid of you for the day anyways." Jack, being good natured, laughed and said. "Your missus called me a few days ago and told me to please get your ass out of her site for a day, she begged me, please, so I took pity on her and agreed." "I guess we are in the same boat then," Byron said as they both laughed. Arthur was enjoying the joking back and forth between his father and Jack and laughing along with them as he hurried, trying to keep up. 'Time for a little rest, ' Byron said as he sat down on a large boulder. "Come sit here next to me" he said as he motioned to Arthur to sit next to him, "you will need some energy for the climb up around the falls to the pond".

Arthur was happy to sit and rest for a while, he was getting tired. Arthur hoped they would be there soon. Jack also found a suitable place to sit. Arthur was, living out his dream. This was the happiest day of his life as he sat next to his father who had his arm around him hugging him close. "This may be as good as it gets," Byron said to Jack, as he held Arthur a little closer. Arthur felt so secure and so happy in those moments sitting next to his father as he leaned into one of his father's big hugs. "What a day Arthur," Byron said, "A day we will never forget."

18

Moose

In the distance they could hear the chirping of birds and what sounded like a rush of running water. After about 10 minutes, Byron stood up and said "okay let's go. "Yes, I can hear the falls, let's go" Jack said. "Arthur strained his ear but he did not hear the falls, the only thing he heard was the sound the river made as it made its way down stream and the bird's chirping nearby. Suddenly Byron stopped, raising his hand up indicating for Jack and Arthur to stop. Byron whispered. A loud cracking and rustling noise could be heard, just up ahead. "It could be a black bear," Jack said as he listened. "I heard there are bears in this area now," he said "but I have never seen one during any of my trips up here." Arthur became very tense and scared, he could feel the butterflies in his belly. He also felt Byron and Jack's apprehension and that made him worry. "If there is a bear we may have to run for it" Byron said in a whisper. Jack was over six feet tall and was a very muscular man, not much scared him, but now he looked worried. "No worries" Arthur, Jack whispered, "If we have to make a run for it, I will grab you with me." I can carry a little fellow like you and your father to if I have to, without even breathing hard," said Jack with a laugh. Then they could hear the sound of crackles in the trees get closer. Bryon motioned his hand to Arthur and Jack to get down into the brush lining the river bank. Byron then motioned for Arthur to come closer to him. Arthur eased up closer to his father. Byron reached back to place his arm around his son to help calm him down. "Don't worry my son," Byron whispered as he placed his arm around him. Arthur felt very secure and safe with his father's calming words.

They stayed in a crouch in the brushes for at least 5 minutes but to Arthur it seemed like an hour without moving as they heard the noise getting closer. All three of them grew very tense as they waited. It must be a bear Arthur thought, "It is too noisy for a small animal." Jack and Byron were ready to spring into action at any moment. Then there was a big splash from the river that startled Byron and Arthur. Jack began to laugh in a big belly laugh. Byron looked at Jack, and cursed him when he realized the splash was from a stone Jack had thrown out into the river.

"You SOB, you trying to give me a heart attack today Jack, "Byron said in an angry tone. "You SOB". Jack just laughed, shaking his head. You have it coming to you for that Jack," Byron said, laughing along with Jack as he realized what Jack was up to.

Suddenly there was movement just a few meters up river as a large bull moose entered the river with a big splash. Byron and Jack seemed amused by the moose but not Arthur, he had never seen such a large animal before. Arthur was amazed by its size and it's seemingly lack of fear of humans. The moose was upwind from the trio so could not get the scent of them. Jack and Byron relaxed and stood up to stare at the moose, they were in awe of its size but had no fear of it. "He is a big ole Bull, probably about a thousand pounds," Byron said. His father and Jack's lack of fear puzzled Arthur because he was so scared his heart was pounding faster. "Arthur no worries, Jack and I have seen many moose, they are just a Newfoundland speed bump is all", his father said with a laugh. The speed bump reference was to how many moose and car accidents that occurred in the province roads yearly. The moose stood in the river just drinking water oblivious to humans, its natural enemy that stood watching nearby. The moose stopped drinking and looked up, slightly turned its head as if listening and smelling something. It gave a snort and a moose call. The moose turned and began trotting down the river toward them, Arthur felt like he was about to crap his pants.

As the moose charged toward them, Jack and Byron started to jump up and down yelling and waving their arms. The moose stayed on its course charging toward them but Byron and Jack stood their ground, showing no fear. Then just as Arthur thought the moose was going to hit them hard it veered left just passing by so close he was sure he felt the wind from the moose on his face. Wow that was close, Byron said as he turned to watch the moose trot down the river then turn right onto the river bank and disappear into the brush. Laughing Jack said, "Arthur, buddy your father and I have to go remove the Johnny cake from our asses now, because we just pooped our pants. Byron said with a grin, "Tell the truth Jack, you crapped your pants when you first saw that big ole bull buddy." "Now" said Byron, "you should go for a dip into the river to wash yourself off buddy". Jack walked toward Byron, grabbed his shoulder and made a pushing motion as if to push Byron into the river. "Not today, " Byron said, moving away from Jack. "You can just frig off". Arthur was enjoying the camaraderie and joking of Jack and his father and it helped relax him.

Motioning up river "Okay let's get going", Jack said. "Yes, let's," Byron said. The group headed up the river toward the falls. Arthur noticed all along the river there were deep pools of swirling water. He liked the sound of the rushing water and the site of the pools as the water swirled around and through them. In some areas he noted there were pools of much calmer water near the river banks that could be great to swim in. "Look at those pools," Byron said, pointing out into the river. 'That would be a great place to catch salmon when the season opens," he said.

19

The Falls

Then Arthur heard something, could that be the waterfall he thought? "Is that the waterfall I hear," Arthur asked his father? Before his father could answer, Jack chimed in, "That my boy is where we are going young fellow," he said.

Arthur could hear the excitement in Jack's voice which made Arthur excited also. Byron looked at his son and said, 'That is the place you have been dreaming about for a long time." open your eyes and really see it, my son, drink it in." Byron slowed down, then stopped just as they rounded a bend in the river. "There it is Arthur! You hear that sound and take in that site. You will never forget this day, your first glance of Red Harbour Falls", said Byron. He continued on to say, "You and I will remember and talk about this day forever, my boy. "I remember the first time I was here with your uncle Nick and uncle Bob. It was a great day that I will never forget."

Arthur really loved his uncle Bob. He spent many days and nights at his uncle's house hanging out with Bob's son Bradley, Arthur's first cousin. Arthur stopped and looked ahead to see the most majestic waterfall he had ever seen. Arthur would never forget this day. As he got closer to the waterfalls, he noticed there was a hard stone ledge high above, over which the gushing water fell, he noticed the water's steep fall over a rocky jagged ledge above. The falling water pulled down by gravity had eroded the rock edges to give the rock a softer glassy look. The water erosion had left a hard ledge over which the water from the pond above fell.

Then about half way down the water splashed over a small rocky ledge whose edges had been worn softer over time by the rushing water. From that ledge the water then continued on down into the river pool below about 30 meters from Arthur. The sun transformed the mist from the water into many little rainbows that danced about the water like fairy dust, as it fell into the plunge pool below. "Wow! What a site, a site that I will never grow tired of," Byron said. "Me neither," said Jack.

Byron held out his arm and gave Arthur a big hug and pulled him closer. Arthur filled up with emotion and a rush of happy tears fell down his face. Aww Arthur, Byron said looking at his son, "it is okay my boy no worries, as he wiped the tears away from his son's face". "Tears are a normal happy emotion my son."

Arthur was so happy and he knew this was a special day with his dad and Jack. Pointing upward, Jack said, "Okay now then, we have to find the trail up around the falls so we can fish in the ponds up there. Arthur was worried as he looked up to see Jack disappear through the brush to start the climb up, what appeared to be a very steep hill. 'Okay Arthur," Byron said 'you go ahead of me I will keep an eye on you from behind as you climb."

Byron and Arthur started the climb. It was a difficult climb through trees and brush but Jack was in the lead and he had climbed this hill many times with Byron. Jack was picking a good path up the steep hill, or at least the best path that could be found. The climb was hard for Arthur.

As Arthur ascended the hill, he struggled. The hill was a steep climb, a hill that seemed like a mountain, but he did not complain. Byron yelled ahead looking up the hill, "Jack, we are taking a break, I do not want the young fellow to get too tired to fish buddy," Jack responded. "Oh! You are getting too old to climb this hill and blaming it on Arthur," Byron had found a comfortable dry spot to sit. Jack came back down to meet them. "Arthur, come over here and sit for a spell," he said, "do not worry about ole Jack he is a little crazy." Arthur, protecting his dad said "I really was getting tired, Jack," "it is a steep hill and I could hear dad breathing harder," Oh, Byron said, "both of you picking on me now".

Arthur looked around him, he could see part of the water falls through the trees and could hear the water rushing down breaking the silence. He was looking forward to seeing the ponds at the top. The ponds he prayed and dreamed about to see and fish since he could remember. Arthur also noticed there were many small but tall spruce trees growing on the hill side. He also noticed the ground was dry probably due the steep slope allowing the rain water to drain away quickly. He also noticed how steep the hill was as he sat, looking back down the hill. "No hurry, we are half way up buddy, we are just going to enjoy the day one moment at a time, we will soak them all in", Byron said. Arthur noticed his father was very calm and really at peace today. Arthur knew his father loved to go fishing at Red Harbour Falls ponds. Yes, ponds, because a few days ago his father had told him, on the other side of the pond above the falls there was a small river. Follow that river about half a km and we would find another pond he had said. "If we have time, we will fish that pond also," It's not good to look too far in the future because that is time God has not given us yet. It's not ours and possibly never will be my son," stated Byron.

Jack stood up, dusted the twigs of his pants, turned and started the climb up the hill again. "Come on boys let's get going." "Byron and Arthur stood up also and started up behind Jack. Jack seemed to be in a hurry now. Jack was anxious to get to the pond to start fishing. As they climbed, Byron reminded Arthur how much he was enjoying himself on this trip. As Arthur climbed he looked around and noticed in some places the ground had slid downhill a few meters. "It looks like the hill is collapsing," Arthur said to his father. Byron chuckled and said, "The slope is steep, when it rains, over time the ground gets soft and gravity pulls it downward, causing the mud topsoil to slide". "I hope it does not totally wash out here because it will slide into the river and could dam the river causing it to re-route, that would not be good."

Just ahead Arthur saw Jack stop and start getting his rod ready "Wow buddy, "Byron said to Arthur, "We are here my son." Arthur and Byron arrived at the top of the hill.

The three fishermen had arrived at the eastern end of the pond near where the pond flowed and changed into a fast flowing short river to flow over the falls into the plunge pool below.

There directly in front of Arthur was the place he had only dreamed about. He was looking at the most beautiful site he had ever seen. Red Harbour falls pond. The place he had only heard about, as described by his father, his uncles and his father's friends. "Look at that, my son, a site for sore eyes," Byron said. "Okay Arthur take a deep breath" Byron said as he breathed in a deep breath and let it out slowly. Arthur noticed the pond was calm. The beauty all around it could be seen with the reflection in the pond. The pond was showing off the beauty around it. As they breathe in and slowly out Arthur and Byron were relaxing their mind and body. Following his father's lead the two breathed in and then out a few times. Jack was heard saying, "Jeepers boys save some air for me." Byron was too busy teaching Arthur to let go of all of the stresses of life, to bother with Jack. They were here now and it was time to relax. Slow life down let the cares and troubles of life go, to be here just in this moment. Arthur knew his father really wanted to relax today and enjoy every minute.

Then Jack, knowing this was a time for father and son, slipped off to the left. Jack looked back saying, "I am going to go fishing around the pond this way boys, I will catch up with you over there," motioning toward the other side of the pond.

Today father and son would have a special day. A day memories that will live on in their memories for many years to come. Arthur was busy following his father's lead, as he took a deep breath then let it out, as he scanned the view before him. The pond was completely calm, the bright morning sun reflected off the water showing off the reflection of the sky, not a ripple could be seen. The surface of the pond was like a glass surface.

In a few areas of the pond, a trout breached the surface, creating ripples that spread out in all directions. 'A good sign, the trout are here this morning," said Byron. Arthur could see his reflection into the clear water of the pond. Across the pond Arthur could see a rocky shore line and waist high brush dotted with low growing evergreen trees. He noted all around the pond there was a rocky shore and in a few places there were trees protruding out to the water's edge.

Just directly across the pond from where he and his father stood. Arthur saw what seemed to be the mouth of a small river. "Just over there is the small river I told you about. "We will follow it up to the next pond if we have time, Arthur," his father said, pointing to the spot.

Arthur could hear the sound of rushing water to his right. Looking over to his right, he realized he was standing just a few meters from the area where the pond started to form a river as it rushed to fill the void at the top of the falls. He saw the water swirl around the many large stones that dotted and helped form the mouth of the falls. At this area the water made a rushing loud swooshing sound and a visible swirling current at the pond's rocky shore line as it rushed to drop over the falls to the river plunge pool below. From the plunge pool it would continue down river.

Byron looked at his son and said," follow me I have something to show you". Arthur followed his father as he walked a short distance along the shore line and turned right toward the top of the falls. His father walked out to a high rocky ledge that the river had formed over many years. "Look down there, this is one of the best views you will ever see". "It will burn into your memory and stay there forever," said his father, as he reached back to grab his son's hand to guide him forward to look over the rocky ledge.

Arthur carefully inched forward as he strained to see what his father wanted him to see. Directly in front of him Arthur could see the water as it disappeared over the edge of the falls to rush to the waiting river below. The water pulled down naturally by the earth's gravitational field formed a spray mist as it fell into the river plunge pool at the base of the waterfall. A spectacular prism of rainbow colors was visible, in its mist. It was morning and the sun was just getting higher in the eastern sky and shone directly into the falling water. The rainbow colors in the mist really impressed Arthur. "Wow dad," Arthur said in an amazed tone of voice. All along the river, Arthur, could see the slope of the land not visible to him before. The land along the river sloped downward toward the river on both sides. The slopes along the river were covered in different types of trees, scrubs and grasses. Arthur followed the river with his eyes as far as he could see until it disappeared from site.

Then Byron said, "Okay Arthur, let's go find a place to light a fire and fish," as he stepped back from the ledge with Arthur by the hand. Arthur hugged close to his dad as they stepped away from the high rocky ledge. Arthur's heart beat gradually returned to normal as he stepped away from the ledge. "I wanted you to experience that view Arthur, a view you will never forget," Byron said.

"That really was something dad, I have always wanted to see that because, I heard you talk about it so often, "Arthur said. "Okay let's just go this way my son," Byron said. Pointing back along shore toward the direction they had come. Byron walked slowly along the edge of the pond with Arthur close at his side.

As Byron walked he seemed to be looking for something. "That looks like a good place to build a fire and make breakfast," he said, pointing to a spot just back from the pond's edge. Arthur noted the spot his father had pointed to had been used for a fire before, probably by his father or other fisherman on visits to this pond. Arthur saw the place his father chose to light a fire had an old tree branch hanging about a half meter above it. "Remembering the conversation he had with his father yesterday Arthur said, "A great spot dad and look, a branch to hang the Billy kettle on, to make tea, just like you told me, we would need". Yes, it's a great spot that Jack, I and some others have used before, "Byron said."

Arthur, let's gather some wood to make a fire buddy," Byron said. Arthur and Byron scurried about gathering dry firewood. When they had gathered a good pile of firewood, Byron said "okay, my son that will be enough for now let's get started." I am starving, " said Arthur. "My son, nothing like a couple of hungry men, let's get started, "said his father.

20

The Boil Up

Arthur watched his father remove steel wool from his backpack. His father had packed it exactly for this purpose, a fire starter he had used on many occasions during fishing trips. Arthur sat on a rock as he watched his father ready things to light the fire. As Arthur sat quietly he heard the quiet of the moment broken only by the sounds of a few chirping birds and the water rushing to fill the void at the mouth of the falls and the rushing of the water as it dropped over the waterfall into the river. The plunge pool at the base of the falls had been formed over many years by the weight of the water rushing down from the pond high above. Arthur scanned his eyes out across the pond. Although he was a young boy, he now understood why his father loved this place. Arthur would also grow to love this place as years passed. In future years Arthur would have many fishing trips here with his dad, a few friends and cousins.

Arthur looked at his dad and in a matter of fact tone stated, "If I have a son when I grow up dad, I think I will bring him here to go fishing with me, and maybe you to dad". "I look forward to that day my son, three generations of Crocker's fishing here all at the same time, father, son, grandson and grandpa." That would be a wonderful day indeed." A day that would be written into our memory forever," his father said. That thought filled Byron with love and pride for his only son. "Arthur fishing is not all about catching trout, it's also about enjoying making memories, friendships, the journey, enjoying nature and enjoying the beauty God has created all around you," said Byron.

"Okay, Arthur watch how I get this fire going so you will know and remember this technique in the future" Byron said in a soft voice. First Byron laid the steel wool spreading loosely with his fingers. He then gathered some small leaves and twigs and stacked them near the formation of stones that were placed there in a circle on previous fishing trips. Byron continued on, removing the water proof matches from the zipped up small pocket in the packsack. He began lighting the steel wool as he talked to Arthur. Arthur was amazed at how the steel wool fired up into a hot glow beneath the stack of dry leaves and twigs as his father's stack burst into a small fire.

Okay Arthur," now the trick is to build the fire slowly adding bigger items as we build the fire to the size we need it to cook breakfast. "You can take over now my son," Byron said pointing to the pile of different sized wood they had gathered. Arthur jumped up from his boulder seat. "Really dad," he explained in a surprised tone. "Yes, you should learn how to do this my boy," said Byron with a smile.

Arthur kneeled near the small fire and began to build the fire with his father's guidance. The fire gradually grew bigger and hotter. "Good job my son, the fire is big enough for now, and you will have to keep feeding it to keep it about that size Arthur."

Then the silence was broken by the voice of Jack. "I saw the smoke, and figured you guys were starting to cook breakfast," Jack said. "You figured right Jack, young Arthur is making a fire just for that purpose",

Byron said. Not wanting to give too much information as all fishermen do. "Just over there, just up around shore I got a few bites," said Jack, pointing toward a small point made up of boulders extending a few meters out into the pond located about a 1000 meters from where he was standing. Byron, looking toward Jack and pointing at Jack's fishing basket, said "I know you are not telling the complete truth, your catch basket seems to be a little heavier." "You got me, I caught a couple small pond trout over there also," laughed Jack, as he reached into his basket to reveal two trout of about 30 cm.

Arthur was impressed as he spoke in a loud voice "Wow." Don't worry about him, my son, we will be catching trout much better than Jack's, soon after breakfast," stated Byron as he continued his chore of cooking breakfast.

From his backpacks Byron took out a container in which he had stored eggs, a zip lock bag full of sliced bologna, and a plastic container he had stored sliced homemade bread to make toast. Byron took out a bag containing a lightweight fry pan, a few plastic plates, a couple of tin mugs and a wire contraption he soon made into a makeshift toaster. He then untied the Billy kettle hanging from his backpack and handed it to Arthur. "Go over to the running water my son, fill the kettle full and bring it back to me buddy, we are going to make tea," Byron said.

As Byron went about getting the tea ready he explained his actions to Arthur so he could see and understand the tradition of making tea, a tradition handed down from his own father many years ago.

Byron had the large backpack and had carried most of the things needed, food, Swiss army knife, can opener, cooking gear, mugs and waterproof, matches, and steel wool to help light the fire, the Billy kettle and any other pots they may need. Byron said, "steel wool would burn well for lighting a fire and was a trick he had learned from his father

A few days ago Byron had removed the lid from a large apple juice can, punched a hole in each side of the can near the top where he added a wire through both sides. He said to Arthur, "on our fishing trip we will use this can as a makeshift kettle, a Billy kettle his father said it was". "We will boil water in it to make our tea." Byron also told his son "we will need a wood branch to lean over the fire, and hang the Billy kettle on that branch over the fire to boil the water for the tea."

"You watch what I do so you can learn how to do this yourself, my son." Byron said. "Your grandfather Crocker used Red Rose loose tea or pound tea in his time because that was all available and we will also". He continued on talking to Arthur," I purchased loose tea at the shop, just for old memories sake. It is difficult to find these days." The night prior to the planned fishing trip Byron packed the backpack. ." Byron went into the forest with his father during winter to cut firewood to use in the family wood stove in their house. Steel wool was a really good cheap fire starter and readily available in those days. "It was light weight to carry and worked great for the purpose. It was the best they could get for fire starter in those days," said Byron.

"Today there are newer types of wide bottom kettles to use for tea making on a fishing trip, but I prefer this method of making tea, a tradition my father taught me," Byron Stated. Byron had learned from his father when he was a young boy like Arthur. "The important thing to remember is to let the water in the Billy kettle boil over twice prior to removing it from the fire as my father taught me," he explained to his son, 'The reason to let the kettle water boil over twice. The first boil over expels the tree dropping, such as bark or pine needles, or whatever debris has dropped into the open top of Billy kettle while it is hanging on the tree branch over the fire". Droppings caused by the wind or the moving about from the cooking. "Normally, "Byron explained, 'my father would find a spot for a small fire that has a tree branch hanging over it or arrange one to hang the kettle". "We used the small wood branch to hang the kettle by the wire hanger, same as I am preparing here." This will allow the heat from the fire to boil the water." Byron went on, "The wire hanger will also allow us to move the kettle to give room to add a frying pan, or a pot. It will also give room for us to remove the boiling kettle safely from the fire so it will not burn or scald anybody."

After hanging the kettle in a good location to boil the tea, Byron continued on with placing a few stones at strategic locations in the fire to place the frying pan. Using a makeshift poker of wood, he moved some of the hot cinders of wood between the stones to set up a place to lay the frying pan to fry the eggs and bologna. He then placed some butter into the frying pan and laid down the pan on the stones just away from direct flames he had prepared. As the butter melted he placed the bologna into the pan first. As the meat fried, Byron readied the toaster with toast and laid it aside on a nearby rock. As the food was cooking Arthur felt hungrier than ever and could not wait to get started eating breakfast. Byron took a long fork out of his bag. "Okay my boy take care of the bologna my son", he said, handing Arthur the fork, "but be careful not to burn yourself or the Bologna." Arthur jumped at the opportunity to help out with the cooking. "Okay no problem dad" Arthur said. Although he was anxious to start fishing Arthur was enjoying the moments of learning to build a fire and make a boil up.

Arthur watched the bologna fry and turned it to ensure both sides were just browned. He removed it from the frying pan and placed it on the plate his father had set aside for that purpose. "Okay my boy I will cook the eggs, because we have to be careful, the fire is hot and they cook quickly," Byron said. He then added some butter and a few eggs to the frying pan. Byron also set up the toast next to the fire. He had already added bread to the toaster to make toast. "Okay guys get a plate and find a place to sit," he said, as he removed the eggs from the pan. Byron added a slice of bologna and two eggs to each plate and one unbuttered slice of toast. "If you want your toast buttered you will have to do it yourself guys," Byron said as he removed the smoking toast from the fire. Darn it burned a little, but it will be okay. 'If you don't like it, then make your own," he said. "Look at you old grumpy self," said Jack. "No, just not your wife," said Byron, with a chuckle, "so get over there and eat," pointing to a big rock that Jack had been sitting on. Okay Arthur you want two eggs or one my son, as his father placed the slice of bologna and an egg on his plate. "Bologna, one egg and a toast,' said Arthur. 'Okay, guys enjoy," said Byron as he loaded up his own plate.

Byron reached in to remove the tea that had started to boil but just before he could remove the kettle from the fire he heard. 'Dad! Let it boil over twice", Arthur shouted. 'True my son, true my son," Byron answered with a knowing grin. He realized his son had been listening to what he had told him, same as he had learned from his own father. Byron waited until the tea had finished boiling over twice just as his son had directed, before removing it from the fire. "Okay Jack, you take care of the tea you lazy arse," said Byron. Byron then turned and walked over to a large rock to sit and started to eat breakfast next to Arthur. Arthur saw his father look at him and wink and let out a chuckle. "It has been a long morning without food, I am hungry', said Byron. "Me too," said Arthur. "Me too," said Jack as he made the tea. Soon the trio were all eating the freshly cooked breakfast and sipping their hot tea.

The sun had risen higher. It was now about 10 A.M. The trio enjoyed the backdrop of the pond with the occasional surface breach of trout and sounds of the waterfall nearby as they ate. As soon as Byron finished his breakfast he got up, washed his plate in the pond and walked over to the fire. Byron poured more tea in his and Jack's mug and passed a mug to Jack. "I brought some sugar and coffee whitener also, help yourselves" said Byron pointing toward a rock where he had laid the tea additives.

Byron took out a cigar from his jacket inside pocket. "I always bring one for this occasion," he said. Byron was not a smoker but when he went fishing he always liked to sit on the edge of the pond at a special place to relax, slow life down and enjoy the moments and scenery around him with an Old Port cigar and a tea. The smoke also helped keep away any misquotes about. Byron reached to pick up a stick of about a foot long and placed the end of it into the fire. He stood and waited until the end of the stick had burst into flame, he then wetted his cigar and placed it into his mouth. He then reached down to remove the stick and the fire walked over to the rock he was sitting on. He sat down on the rock, raised the burning stick toward his face to light the cigar. Byron puffed on the cigar as the smell of the cigar filled the morning air all around them.

Byron got really comfortable as he puffed on his cigar in one hand and his tea in the other. He looked around him and said, "This is as good as it gets my boys." Byron sat down to relax for a while, he noticed a slight warm breeze had come up blowing from the South West. The breeze made the blue water of the pond look like diamonds dancing on the water. He had to squint his eyes to protect them from the bright sun reflecting off the water. Byron, fished his sunglasses from his pocket.

Just across the pond on the other side Byron noticed the shore line had an intermittent gravel and rocky shore. Occasionally the shore gave way to a clump of brush crowding the pond's edge. He could also see many trees, a combination of low growth evergreens and spruce. Byron could not see what type of trees they were from his vantage point but he knew because he had fished from that edge of the pond and knew the type of trees in that area, As he looked just above the tree line past the trees he could see a sky that included a few grayish white clouds across the horizon in the distance as if painted by the strokes of a painters brush. As Byron puffed on his cigar and drank in the scene before him, the sound of the waterfall was the only sound to break the silence of the beautiful morning air. The trio sat in silence

Arthur was uncomfortable with all the silence. He was enjoying his breakfast and tea but was anxious to get started. After all, his biggest dream was to come here to fish with his father, not sit around eating and talking. Arthur was trying hard to be patient but really was wanting to get trout fishing

"You know Arthur, sometimes words are not necessary, silence can be golden, one day you will realize, silence really does have a sound," his father said. Byron continued to drink in the view before him as he puffed on his cigar. After a few minutes he stood up, removed the fire from the cigar and tossed it into the pond to ensure it would not cause a forest fire and said "I will save the remainder for later my son." Use the kettle and pour water into the fire Arthur. We have to ensure any fire is extinguished, we do not want to start a forest fire and spoil this place. "Okay dad, let's go fishing, "Arthur said. "Yes it is about time you started to move, the young fellow is bored, he came here to fish, so get him ready to fish," said Jack with a laugh. "You make yourself useful Jack, help extinguish the fire," Byron ordered.

Jack went about ensuring any fire was totally extinguished grumbling a little as he went about his chore. Arthur, eager to start fishing, jumped up and started to clean up. He went to the water's edge and kneeled to reach into the water to wash his hands, his plate and his mug.

21

Peaceful Joy

Arthur and his father were ready to fish as soon as breakfast was finished. "Are you going fishing today, Jack quipped?" "You keep your big mouth shut Jack," said Byron laughing, "we are ready for fishing, we have already prepared our fishing rods." Both Arthur and Byron had a brand of fishing gear referred to as Mitchell Rods and Mitchell open face reels." An open face reel is best for fishing Byron had told his son some time ago. Arthur heard his father say," An open face reel is easier to make a cast out into the water and better to control any line tangling or snarls."

The first task of preparing fishing gear, Byron had performed when they first arrived at the pond. He ensured Arthur's fishing rod and his own were ready for fishing. After assembling the fishing rod, Byron taught Arthur how to tie a hook to the end of the nylon fishing line, and said, "We will add the bobber later, about a half meter from the hook depending on the dept. of the water." He then showed Arthur the art of feeding a worm onto the hook. Learning to feed a worm on the hook was a slower process for Arthur because he had to learn not to pierce his fingers in the process. Byron advised his son, saying "you will improve with more experience and gain confidence in your abilities."

In preparation for the fishing trip, Byron had taught Arthur how to place the fishing line on the fishing reel spool a few days earlier by performing the task himself on his own reel then coaching Arthur to fill his own fishing reel spool. Arthur enjoyed learning to take care of his own fishing gear. This task made Arthur more excited about his much anticipated fishing adventure. 'Okay," he said "The next important thing to learn is, get a worm from the bait box and I will show you how to bait your hook'. Arthur watched intently as his father baited the hook. Byron took all the time necessary for Arthur to learn the procedure of feeding the bait onto the hook. He then said "I think you will need a bobber on your line first to learn the art of trout fishing" so he got a bobber from our fishing tackle box and taught him how to tie it and at the correct location that would keep the hook the right distance above the pond bottom to allow him to catch trout. After they finished that procedure, he said "understand when a trout bits your hook, trying to steal your worm the bobber will move". Arthur, at that very moment, you have to give a quick tug on the rod," he said, motioning the fishing rod with his arms". He then set the fishing rod in Arthur's hands showing him the proper way to hold a rod and how to cast the line out into the pond, the same procedure he had taught him a few days ago, now was just a refresher as he referred to it as. "If you are lucky you will catch your first fish today my boy," he said with a chuckle. Byron found and set his young son up where he thought was a good place, a spot where he had caught fish many times before. Now he said,' you can just leave your line in the water and help me, but keep an eye on your bobber just in case you get a bite. Arthur stated in a matter of fact tone of voice "No I think I will just fish for now", "Oh, okay, "Byron said as he walked away to get his own gear ready for fishing. As Byron got ready for fishing he lit his cigar, sat down on a large rock and motioned for his son to come sit next to him. Then as Arthur walked toward his father he remembered his fishing line was still out into the pond. He sat next to his father and reeled in his line to look at the hook but no fish was there. It's okay to cast out your line when you have a bobber on it and just let it sit until you see it moving by a possible trout biting the hook," Byron advised his son. "Oh, okay dad no problem, "Arthur said. Standing up, He casted his line, bobber and hook back out into the pond, as far as he possibly could.

Arthur was a very happy young man to be with his dad today on the rocky shores of Red Harbour Falls Pond. A fishing trip to the place that he thought was a mystical place during the times he heard his father talk about it. A place that Arthur knew was his dad's most favorite place to go fishing. Now, here he was at a place he had only dreamed about for such a long time. Byron smiled at Arthur and said," A little piece of heaven this place is."

Arthur's father seemed so much at peace in those moments as they sat looking out over the pond. The only sound that could be heard was the water rushing over the falls and the occasional trout jumping in the lake leaving a ripple of water spreading out in a circle and gradually dissipating into nothing. As the young boy saw some trout jump and suspend into the air he got excited and wanted to go cast his line into that area of the ripple. Then his father said, 'it will not be here when your hook arrives at that spot.' "There is no hurry, there is lots of time to fish today, my son. "He understood his son's excitement to catch a fish, his first one. To Arthur it seemed time was standing still.

Arthur noticed his father was so relaxed and peaceful today, it was a valuable lesson he would always remember. Enjoy the moments we have one at a time and enjoy the others as they come and do not rush them. Arthur, although just a boy, seemed to understand that today would mean much more as time passes. Those moments sitting on the shores of Red Harbour falls pond having breakfast and then fishing with dad would be a cherished memory. Byron was looking out over the pond when Arthur noticed what appeared to be a tear trickling down his father's cheek. Arthur did not know at the time but Byron was remembering a much happier time with his own dad who had passed when he was just thirteen years old.

Arthur asked "are you okay dad"? "Yes" his father said, "think that was a drop of rain that fell on my face," as he wiped it off with the back of his hand. Arthur thought, "That's odd because it is sunny and no clouds were in the sky. Certainly no rain was falling."

22

Finally

Deep in thought, Byron said, "my son, we do not have forever, that is why we have to enjoy every day God gives us." Arthur's father was very relaxed and methodical in his approach to fishing, no rush. A lesson the boy would take into his adult years. This memory would always be a great memory of his dad as years passed.

As the years passed Arthur would go fishing with others or alone. At those times his mind would wander back to remember those special days he and his dad spent together trout fishing at Red harbour falls Ponds and the raindrop on his father's face that appeared without a cloud in the sky, now he understood that very special moment. Those days could never be replaced in his memory. Arthur would always have those fond memories to look back on.

Arthur stood at the edge of the pond about 5 meters from his father. He knew two people fishing near each other needed to keep some space between them to ensure room for casting their line out into the pond for fishing. The space would also help to prevent entanglement of the fishing lines.

With all the strength he had, Arthur casted his fishing line with the attached baited hook and bobber as far into the pond as he possibly could. He then waited patiently watching his bobber for any sign of a trout biting his hook. Arthur had to squint his eyes to shield them from the bright sun reflecting off the pond's blue water. The water was blue due to the reflection of the beautiful blue sky above on this gorgeous warm sunny Newfoundland morning. He felt so happy and peaceful as he fished. 'What a day," he thought! He glanced intermittently toward his father for reassurance. Byron was casting his line out into the pond much further than Arthur. Byron was wearing sun shades to protect his eyes from the sun glare of the water. "I need a pair of sunglasses," Arthur thought. "I will do that also when I get bigger," Arthur said under his breath". Arthur's eyes wandered back to his own bobber out in the water. He did not want to miss a fish he thought, not wanting to look away for more than a few seconds.

Then, there it was Arthur's bobber dipping with the tug of a fish biting at his hook. It was after his bait. Arthur sprang into action and knew just what to do as he motioned his rod to the side with a sharp quick tug. He was going to catch that fish. Arthur had played this moment over in his mind many times.

Now was the time to place into action, what he had been taught. As the drag on his line kept a slight steady strain on the rod and line, his bobber went under water. Arthur felt and saw his fishing rod bend in his hands as he felt the tug of the fish trying to swim away with his hook and bait in its mouth. Arthur had hooked his first fish. It's a big one, he thought. He felt the rush of excitement go through his body as he let out a yell. "I got one Dad.

Arthur kept a steady strain on his line and hook because his line drag had been set for just this moment to successfully reel in his first ever fish. 'You sure do have one,' Byron shouted with glee," as he watched his son reel in his first fish. "Don't rush it buddy" Byron said. Byron then let out a breath and relaxed, as he watched Arthur reel in his first fish. Arthur continued to reel in, keeping a strain on the hooked fish to ensure it would not wiggle off the hook and escape back into the pond. "He's a fighter," yelled Byron as he rushed over to watch Arthur. The excitement of the moment could clearly be heard in Arthur's voice as he shouted, "Yes and a big one dad." Having experienced fishing this pond many times, Byron knew there were not any fish in this pond much bigger than 25 or 30 cm, but shared in Arthurs excitement as he shouted," I think you are right my son."

This was Arthur's first fish and of course like any fisherman, fish usually seem bigger than they really are. Fish usually grow in size during the retelling of a fishing story. When retelling fishing stories the story can become a Pinocchio like story with fish growing in size and numbers each time the story is told. This story would be no different as time marched on.

The fish broke the surface of the water just a few feet from the shore, wiggling with all the strength it could muster to escape its prison. The fish gleamed silver and black as the sun reflected off its wet scaly skin.

Then just as Arthur was about to give his rod a quick tug to land the fish onto the pebble beach around his feet, the fish wiggled free of the hook prison that held it. Arthur watched in horror as the fish swam back out into the pond as fast as it could, none the worst for its ordeal it seemed. "Oh no," Arthur exclaimed," It got away." Arthur felt the pings of disappointment. A disappointment that hurt more than anything he had ever felt. Arthur's eyes welled up with tears, He looked to his father, and showed his frustration and disappointment. What would his dad say now? As his father looked on, he felt his son's disappointment but was quick to give reassurance to his son. "No worries, buddy you will catch and also lose many fish as you get experience, we all have. "Arthur felt disappointed and sad as he watched his trout escape his hook but felt a little better from his father's reassurance. Fathers can choose to yell foolish comments of stupidity or words of encouragement at times like these. Byron knew there were going to be many future exciting fishing times and some disappointments ahead, in his son's fishing future. Byron knew Arthur would learn to be a better fisherman from his mistakes just as he had growing up, while fishing with his father, his brothers and his friends.

After a few more minutes fishing, Arthur yelled, "I have another one on dad." Byron looked on with pride as his son reeled in his trout, this time landing it safely on the beach behind him. "Hmm," Byron said softly," out loud to himself just out of earshot of Arthur, "he has learned from his previous experience of losing the trout just a few minutes ago.' Arthur will always remember the experience of losing his first trout.

A mistake is an important lesson learned that is valuable in gaining experience for the long term. Byron remembered a comment said to him once by his boss. Show me a fellow that does not make a mistake and I will show you somebody not doing anything. Byron wanted his son to take responsibility for his own mistake and learn from it. It was obvious to Byron, Arthur had learned from his mistake as he watched him reel in more fish. He was learning fast how to become a good fisherman.

Arthur was gaining valuable experience as the day passed. As the day passed Byron would watch as Arthur lost more fish off his hook, just muttering to himself. Byron smiled to himself at his son's muttering. Byron noted his son never asked for help with his fishing. He wanted to be independent and was improving greatly as he figured it out himself as the day wore on.

The pair, father and son continued to fish and chat as they made their way around the pond. Byron stopped once to make a fire and tea, a boil up. It was coming up for lunch when Byron lit the fire a second time and said to his son. "Arthur, I think we will clean a few trout for a fry up for lunch, come over and I shall show you what to do. Byron reached in his pocket and took out his Swiss army pocket knife. "Okay, my son, take a few trout, about 10, and wash them in the pond water, when you are done lay them on that flat rock over there on the bank," Byron said pointing to the nearby bank of the pond.

Arthur did exactly as his father asked. Byron then walked over to the trout Arthur had placed on the flat rock. He then took the blade of his knife starting at the tail slid his knife blade up through the belly of the fish stopping just at the head. He then removed the belly from the trout leaving the head attached. Arthur looked on intensely." Okay now take the trout and wash them in the pond and clean them well Arthur," Byron said. Byron then took a plastic bag of flour mixed with salt, pepper and a few herbs from his backpack, an ingredient he had prepared last night just for this moment. "Okay, Arthur, let's add one trout at a time to this bag and shake to coat it with the flour and herb mixture. When he was done Arthur placed each trout on a plate to wait until his father was ready to fry them."

Byron then removed his frying pan from the back pack and added some butter to it, as he placed it on the fire. "The butter will add flavor," he said. "Wait a minute, Arthur, for the pan heat up before you put trout into the pan." Soon Arthur had the trout sizzling in the pan as the heat and butter turned them to a beautiful golden brown. "The trout will only be a couple minutes cooking so be careful not to burn them," said Byron.

As soon as they were cooked Arthur removed the trout from the pan with the spatula and placed them on the stone near the fire to stay warm. Arthur had checked the flat rock with his bare hand and noted it was warmed by the nearby flames. Within a few minutes the trout were cooked and ready to eat. "Great job Arthur," his father said. Arthur was excited to start eating. This was the first time he had cooked his own fish he himself had caught.

Arthur was continuing to make memories with his dad he would have for his lifetime. Byron took out two plates and added five trout to each plate plus a slice of homemade buttered bread. Arthur mother made her own bread. He would not have to eat store purchased manufactured baked bread until he left home for university. They dug in, no more words were necessary. Arthur proudly looked at his dad and said, "This fish is really tasty and probably the best fish I have ever eaten." As they finished eating Byron said, "Arthur, that was good buddy, "The Best I have ever had dad," Arthur felt very happy just in that moment. Looking across the pond Arthur could see Jack had a fire burning also. Dad, Jack is having a boil up to he stated. "Oh yes, Jack can take care of himself", he enjoys these trips just as much as I do," his father confirmed.

Byron made ready a cup of tea for himself, but Arthur did not want any tea. "Okay now to finish my cigar," Byron said, as he reached into the fire and withdrew a burning stick to light the half of the cigar he had left from the morning boil up. Byron sat down on the shore and puffed on his cigar while sipping his tea. These were the moments Byron really loved and hoped his son would grow to love. Learn to slow life down and enjoy the peacefulness of getting away fishing just enjoying the quiet and calmness all around. " This is as good as it gets my son, "Byron said as he sucked in and let out a big breath. "God has created such beauty", he said," We just have to learn to see and enjoy the beauty all around, just as he created it.

23

Gratitude

 The pair continued fishing along the leeward side of the pond catching a few fish as they moved along. Two hours later they arrived at the place where a small river flowed into the pond. Arthur's father had pointed out this spot across the pond this morning when they arrived. "Okay my son we will fish this river until we get to the pond just a few hundred meters from here," Byron Said. Arthur noted the brook was fairly wide and had a pebble beach along its bank, easy to fish from. Arthur went ahead of his dad up the small river, keeping far enough ahead to ensure no line tangles occurred with the two fishing lines. Fishing the river was fun for Arthur and much different then pond fishing. He had to be careful not to get tangled in the brush branches overhanging the small river and the trout were much smaller and very quick
 As the pair moved up the river the river's banks became covered in low lying brush difficult to walk through and making it more difficult to fish from it's shore. Byron stated, "okay my son let's get going up to

the next pond. Soon they had the next pond in view and there at the edge on the pond was Jack who had already arrived and was fishing.

The pond in view Arthur felt again a charge of excitement run through his body. This pond Arthur noticed was much smaller than the first pond they left behind. Across the pond there appeared to be a small brook running into the pond. The Sun was high in the sky indicating it was about 2 P.M. Time was rushing by it seemed.

The water was calm and trout were jumping to catch the bugs just above the surface of the water. Arthur felt so happy and at peace within, just loving these moments with his dad and Jack. His dream came through and his many prayers were answered. Jack looked over his shoulder to see his buddies approaching. "Jeepers, I can't go anywhere without you finding me to steal my trout," said Jack as he turned to face them with a loud chuckle. "Any trout Jack," said Arthur. "That's none of your business," said Jack, giving Arthur a big grin and turning to wink at Byron. "I got a few I suppose," Jack said," but nothing to brag about." "Oh, you would not brag until we got home anyway Jack," said Byron. "Who me, never, unless I needed to have a laugh," said Jack. Arthur enjoyed his father and Jack's banter back and forth. "Awe shut up Buddy, get on fishing you have a lot of catching up to do," said Jack with a mischievous look and grin toward Arthur. "Okay," Arthur said laughing, "maybe I will stay with you for a while Jack and you can show me how you fish."

Byron's impatience was showing as he started to walk up around the pond to a spot he had fished many times before. "Okay boys, let's get fishing, we only have an hour or so left before we have to head home, enough of your crap Jack, and don't warp the young fellows mind buddy."

Arthur stayed with Jack and watched his dad walk away alone. Suddenly Arthur became worried and thought, "What if, dad says next time, I cannot come because I decided to stay with Jack." A concerned Arthur stood on the shore of the pond and noted this pond seemed to be more shallow then the first pond. He adjusted the length of line from the hook to the bobber shorter to avoid hook ups. Jack watched on as Arthur adjusted his lead line length. "You are learning fast young fellow." "Of course he knows what to do Jack, I trained him," yelled Byron.

Those words from Jack and his dad made Arthur stand taller and feel much better as he puffed out his chest a little further Then, in less than a minute Arthur yelled," I got one' as he reeled in a fish and flicked it onto the shore. Arthur struggled to unhook the fish from the hook. "Good job Arthur," yelled his father," you are showing that old fellow how to catch a fish". "I just trained him," said Jack laughing, "He is a better fisherman than you will ever be." "Ha, better than you for sure," Byron yelled back.

"Dad has all the fish I caught, in his fish basket," Arthur informed Jack just as his father arrived back to where Arthur and Jack were fishing. Byron looked at his son lovingly, "I thought it was best for me to carry the fish buddy, "that made it better for you to walk and to fish without the weight around your shoulders." Jack suddenly said, "Okay get your rods ready and let's head back down to the other pond boys, don't seem like there is much here to catch."

Within a few minutes the trio were headed back to the first pond at the top of the waterfalls, with Jack leading the way. "A waste of time to go back down that brook, "said Jack. With Jack leading the way they followed a path that bypassed the route they had followed up to the second pond.

In about five minutes of walking, following Jacks through some low growing trees and some brush they arrived at the first pond. The pond had a few ripples on it from a light breeze from the south east. The pond was quiet, so quiet it hurt Arthur's ears. After a few minutes the only sound was his father's voice saying, "okay Jack, "let's split up and we will go around the pond in the opposite direction as before because I want to have a few flicks from some of my favorite fishing spots." "No need, said Jack," I caught all the fish on that side of the pond buddy." Byron winking at Arthur said, "you only caught the small ones, Jack",

" I think there is a big one over there waiting for Arthur, "Byron said," pointing to a place about half way between where they were standing and the waterfalls on the far side. Arthur felt the excitement build in his chest and belly, "Let's get going," Arthur said, already readying his fishing rod and walking toward the place his dad had pointed out.

The trio split up with Jack heading around the pond to the left alone and Byron and Arthur heading to the right, in the opposite direction they had fished earlier in the day. "Okay boys, I will see you over at the falls in about 45 minutes, then we will head home," said Jack. "You seem to be in a bigger hurry today, Jack, the misses must have promised you a special treat when you get home, " Byron said.

As the father and son duo headed out to the opposite side of the pond, there was no banter of voices breaking the silence. There was just father and son stopping to fish occasionally. Arthur had learned his dad liked to fish without talking very much, he seemed to enjoy the silence. Byron was silent but deep in thought, thinking about a valuable lesson he could teach his son on their fishing trip together.

Then, as Byron looked out across the pond he noted; the water was very still, a thought of the rippling effect of a stone came into his mind. "I have it", Byron said out loud to himself. Byron stopped, waited for his son to come closer. He placed his arm around his son's shoulders. He picked up a small stone and threw it out into the pond. " Arthur stood next to his father, feeling his father's love and closeness as he watched the stone cause ripples that spread outward in a circle reaching far beyond where the stone had entered the water. "Do you remember hearing the priest talk about the bible story of an old woman who gave two coins as an offering after a sermon given by Jesus, Byron asked? "Yes I do dad,' stated Arthur. Arthur had gone to the local Catholic Church with his mom and dad since he could remember and had heard the priest talk about that bible passage a few times,

"Well son his father went on to say. Jesus noticed her gift. "I like to compare her actions of giving her two coins all she had; to when a pebble is dropped into still water. Those coins she gave sent out many tiny waves, rippling out from its center where it was dropped. That ripple of that pebble being dropped reaches out far beyond the place where it landed in the water.

That woman's one action had far reaching effects it created a time ripple. Same as when we do kind acts for others. When we are kind with kind words or deeds to others. Our kindness has a ripple effect outward like the stone dropping in the pond. The effects of our actions can reach far beyond their intended target, far beyond our own comprehension.

When we give with an open hand and open heart the effect can spread to other people who in turn spread it to others. The ripple effect for that one exchange may be carried for weeks, months and possibly even years to come.

In the old woman's case, the ripple effect of her actions has continued on for at least two thousand years and is still rippling outward, as energy in motion that is still affecting millions of people. The same can happen when you show kindness and give to others with an open kind heart" said Byron, squeezing his son tighter.

That story as told to him by his dad when he was such a young boy helped make Arthur the kind hearted and generous man Arthur grew up to be.

The air had a hint of coolness of the coming evening and there was complete silence except his father's soft reassuring voice. Byron felt very proud of his son as he told his story and felt Arthur's relaxed state as he looked down to see him listening intensely, just hanging on to every word his father spoke.

Byron said, "Okay, buddy let's try our luck here. On this point I have had a lot of luck catching fish." You go ahead and try while I light another cigar," as he found a place to sit and relax on a big flat boulder located near the water's edge.

Arthur watched as his father lit a cigar he reserved for his special moments. Arthur baited his hook and casted his line out into the pond as far as he possibly could, while his father looked on. A few seconds after Arthur's line and bobber landed into the water, his bobber disappeared from sight. "I think I have a big one dad," Arthur shouted in an excited voice. Arthur felt the pull on his rod. He gave his rod and the line a quick tug to set the hook into the mouth of the fish on the other end of his line. Arthur had set the drag on his reel to a setting that allowed his line to tighten, giving room for the fish to swim away with the hook in its mouth without breaking free of the hook. As the fish began to swim out into the pond to escape its prison, Arthur began to slowly reel his catch in; - to ensure the fish stayed attached to his hook. "Okay buddy take your time, it seems you have a good size fish hooked buddy", yelled Byron. Byron watched with pride as Arthur reeled his fish toward shore. Soon the trout was visible at the water surface as Arthur played it out. The silver belly of the fish was visible as it came closer to shore under Arthur's skill and watchful eye. "You have a good one buddy," Arthur's father exclaimed. Father and son watched as the fish kept wigging to free itself from the hook. Arthur slowly played out his fish as he reeled it in. Soon the trout was close enough to shore to allow him to land it onto the pond's sandy shore.

Wow! - I have the biggest one today Dad," Arthur shouted as he admired his catch". "You sure do Arthur," his dad shouted. The trout Arthur had landed was about 45 CM long and weighed about 2 and a half lbs. Like all fisherman stories, the trout's size would increase every time Arthur and his dad would tell the story of Arthur's big catch. The story is about Arthur catching the biggest fish on his first fishing trip to Red Harbour falls ponds. "You will have to brag about that one to Jack," said his father.

Arthur looked across the pond to see Jack on the other side, waving his arms and beckoning them to come over to where he was. "I think Jack wants to get going home, dad," Arthur said, pointing over to Jack. "Yep, he seems to be in a hurry to get home today, must be something he has to do at home," Arthur. "Let's get going buddy to shut him up," said Byron with a chuckle. The pair continued on their walk to the other side of the pond without stopping to fish along the way.

As the pair approached Jack, Arthur shouted an excited tone "I got a big one over there,' pointing to the area across the pond where he had caught his big fish. "Oh, let's see buddy," said Jack. "You are too small to catch anything big, your father must have caught it and given it to you," said Jack jokingly. He viewed Arthurs catch then Jack went on to say, "Your father probably told you to say you caught it". "No Jack, he caught it on his own rod, although, I would like to take credit for that one, I cannot, "Byron said. Jack looked amazed as he said, "Arthur is becoming quite the good fisherman." "Yes he is, better than both of us," stated Byron, patting his son gently on the head. Arthur felt so proud of himself. He was very happy he had landed the biggest fish of the day. A fish Arthur would brag about for years to come, the day he caught a fish bigger than Jack and his dad during his first fishing trip to Red Harbour falls pond. Today was even better than Arthur had dreamed about in his day and night dreams.

24

Nature's Jacuzzi

Byron said "Okay lets head home," as he walked toward an opening that led to the path back down to the river below the falls. Jack and Arthur followed closely behind Byron. About 10 meters from the pond, Byron looked back at Arthur and stated, "Okay my son just follow Jack and I down the steep embankment to the river and please stay close ". I will not go down straight to avoid any of us slipping or falling." "Get going Arthur, just follow your father and you will be okay and I will follow you," said Jack. Byron started the descent as Arthur watched him slowly zig zag back and forth holding on to any brush or trees in his path down the hill. Slowly the trio made their way down the steep incline. Arthur followed close behind his dad being careful not to go too quickly to avoid slipping or falling. Along the way down Arthur noted the falls, he could hear as the rushing water fell down in the direction of the river below toward where they were headed. In less than twenty minutes the trio stood near the bottom of the falls. At the edge of the deep pool where the falls had carved a hole due to the water erosion over many years.

Arthur looked toward Jack who was busy removing his cloth down to his under shorts. Arthur's father was following Jack's lead. "We usually have a soak here before we go home Arthur," Bryon said. You just go over to the bottom edge of the pool where water flows into the river said Jack. Arthur heard the splash of water as his father and Jack jumped into the water pool.

Arthur looked around to find an area of the river much shallower than where his dad and Jack had jumped in. Arthur was a little embarrassed about removing his cloth and was not in any hurry to do so. He heard his dad and Jack laughing and talking about how warm the water was and how good it felt after a long day fishing in the hot summer sun. The water pool was now in the shade of the falls and the many trees near the river.

Arthur slowly removed his cloth and eased into the warm river water, and it felt so good just sitting in the warm slow bubbling rush of the water passing by. It felt like what Arthur had envisioned a Jacuzzi might feel like. Arthur had never been in a Jacuzzi before, but had seen one at the local furniture store. The water was warm, and the bubbling water of the river was very relaxing. Byron and Jack had found a hidden ledge just under the waterfall and were sitting there just letting the water rush over them as they relaxed. Arthur was thinking his dad and Jack had done this before, because they knew where the water was deepest and where the hidden rock ledge was located. "You want to join us," Byron yelled to Arthur. Arthur could barely hear his dad over the sounds of the water falls and the rushing bubbling river water. Arthur was not brave enough yet to join his dad under the falling water but would try it another day during a future fishing trip with his dad and two cousins Gerard and Bram.

After about twenty minutes Jack and Byron got out of the water. After exiting the river Arthur heard his father say it's chilly now, we are in a shaded area. Jack proceeded to remove his wet under shorts. 'I am getting out of those wet shorts, and just going commando for the walk home," said Jack laughing. Following Jack's lead, Byron took off his wet under shorts to replace them with his dry jeans also. As Jack and Byron, were in the process of changing. Arthur also got out of the river and felt the chill of the shaded area. "Okay, my son, take off your wet underwear and put on your dry cloth for the walk home," said Byron. Arthur was not too comfortable being naked in front of his dad and Jack. Arthur grabbed his cloth and headed toward a bush to cover his nakedness and change his cloth. Byron and Jack looked at each other and chuckled as Arthur disappeared behind a bush to change. Arthur felt more comfortable changing behind the bush and was thankful his dad and Jack did not make a big deal about it.

25

Going Home

The trio gathered their stuff for the walk home. Each carried their own fishing rods. Jack and Byron would carry the two backpacks, one each and the fish. Byron also carried the fish Arthur had caught. "Not a bad day Jack, Arthur caught a dozen trout and the biggest fish and I caught a two dozen, for a total of three dozen," Byron said proudly. Byron placed his arm around Arthur holding him in a big hug of support to show him he was very proud of him. Byron went on to say, "There are only twenty four in the fish basket though, because we fried a dozen for lunch at the pond. "Sure you did boys," said Jack looking at Arthur with a nod and a wink. "Yes we did Jack,' Arthur stated in support of his dad. "I have heard all the Crocker fish stories lies before," said Jack laughing, "okay guys let's get going," as he headed down river with Arthur and Byron following. The trio moved along with Jack leading, Arthur second and Byron third because he wanted to keep a look out for Arthur and help him along where he would need help navigating the trek down river.

The hike back down the river was uneventful. Arthur felt much more comfortable now with his dad and Jack after a day fishing, finally fulfilling his dream of fishing at the Red Harbour falls pond. Arthur thought, "I could walk up to the falls now myself if I wanted to." Arthur was feeling more confident and happy then he could remember. He had matured some today. For Arthur, today was everything he had dreamed about and more. "I will be back," he told himself. He could not wait to get home to tell his mom, his sister and his friends about his first fishing trip with dad. "Just wait until I show them the biggest fish I caught, "he thought.

After about an hour of walking, Jack turned to lead them away from the river and up through the narrow path toward Jack's SUV. This path was partly overgrown with miscellaneous brush, blueberry bushes, and some long grass and over hanging branches of trees.

Arthur also noticed along the way a few pitcher plants, affectionately known as Newfoundland's provincial plant. Arthur had been taught in school about the provincial plant.

Jack arrived at his SUV first. Jack began opening up the doors and windows to cool it down before getting inside for the drive home. As Byron and Arthur arrived, Jack opened up the hatch at the back of the SUV. Byron and Arthur placed their equipment inside the SUV alongside Jack's gear. "A great day Jack my old friend, we will do it again soon," said Byron.

Jack got into the driver's seat and Arthur was told to get in the front seat next to Jack because he caught the biggest fish. "Are you sure Jack, "Arthur asked? "Yes buddy, your father can sit in the back, he deserves it for not catching the biggest fish," laughed Jack. Byron got in the back seat and smiled as he noticed his son's new found confidence and pride in his accomplishment. "You did well today Arthur, I am proud of you," said Byron as Jack drove away down the side road toward the main highway. Arthur sat quietly with his thoughts, about the day he had. A day he would not forget. As Jack made a right turn onto the main road, Arthur felt excited and was thinking about how pleased his mom was going to be with him when he got home. He would tell her about the wonderful day he had fishing at Red Harbour falls pond. They were headed for home.

Jack made the turn into their home driveway. Arriving home Arthur was so excited. Arthur could hardly wait for Jack to bring the SUV to a stop. As the SUV drove up, Agnes came out the door to welcome her boy's home. Jack stopped and Arthur looked toward Jack, "Thanks Mr. Jack, for the day then he bolted out the door toward his mother who had come outside as soon as she saw them turn into the driveway. Byron watched as Agnes put her arm around Arthur and went inside. "He had such a great day Jack," Byron said. One he will never forget, buddy said Jack.

Byron and Jack got out of the SUV. Jack opened the back hatch to let Byron get the fishing gear Arthur and Byron had stored there for the drive home.

"Thanks Mr. Jack, see you soon," Byron said with a grin. Byron entered the house to hear Arthur's animated excited voice telling his mom about his day. Byron went over to his wife, gave her a big hug. Byron and Agnes just stood there with arms locked around each other as they listened to Arthur's story, about his day. As Arthur finished talking, Agnes looked at her son with so much pride and said, "Wow, Arthur you sure had a wonderful day and I really missed my men around here," as she gave both her men a hug, "You are such a good dad and husband for giving him a day he will not soon forget," she said.

It had been almost three months since Byron had been transferred from the hospital to the Rehabilitation center. Arthur had visited his dad every day during his stay here. Sitting in the hair next to his hospital bed. Byron said," Arthur, do you remember the time we took Madison fishing just so we could give her a day out with us fishing. It was not Red Harbour falls because she was so little at the time but she thought it was the place we would go fishing. She had a great day." "Yes I do", said Arthur. A few days later Billy and I told her that was not the place dad took me. I was sorry about it because she was so upset and disappointed after I told her," said Arthur with a grin.

Today was the eighty-seventh day Byron was an inmate, at the Nova Scotia Rehabilitation center located in the South end of Halifax. Byron jokingly referred to his hospital stay as being an inmate. Arthur had sat next to his father's hospital bed for hours every evening, since his father had been stricken with a massive stroke. Although the stroke was almost three months ago; it seemed like a lifetime ago.

Arthur had helped his dad with rehabilitation on a daily basis. Arthur and Louise had been big part of his daily progress. Arthur had grown into a kind gentle man and still remembers that first fishing trip with his dad up the Red Harbour River to Red Harbour falls pond.

Then the door of Byron's hospital room opened. At the door was Byron's doctor with his fiancé Louise and daughter Madison. The doctor came over to sit on the chair next to Byron. "We called the rest of your family to come in for a meeting, because we wanted them to be here for the greatest news we have for you. He went on to say, "I have great news for you and your family.

"Byron, I know you want to stay here but your rehabilitation recovery here is completed now." Byron you can go home in a couple days as soon as we get you ready to understand and accept the challenges ahead of you as you continue your recovery." The doctor went on to say, "while you do that, it is best for you to be at home with the people who love you and will take care of you better than us here at the hospital" Byron got out of his bed and stood up. All four of them embraced with joy at this great news.

Byron looked at Arthur, "Thanks my son, I guess we will have to continue our conversations at home now." Byron gave Madison a hug and kissed her cheek, "thanks honey I know you have been busy with the baby, my new granddaughter Ireland and you have done the best you could

Byron then turned to Louise, put his arms around her with a big hug and a kiss and said, "Thanks for everything honey". Filled with gratitude, Byron looked at his family and stated, "I do not know what I would have done without all of you. Please, go home now, relax, get some great sleep and please do not return here until it is time for me to go home. You guys need a break from here. Now go on, get out of here."

Byron was now left to his thoughts in the quiet of a hospital room, as he watched his family leaving to go home. He knew he was not fully recovered yet. He would have to lean on them for many months ahead. It was a scary time for him because he had never had to depend on anybody since he left home at seventeen years old.

Authors Update

I published my first book threading The Needles of Life in 2017 just a couple years after the brain injury. A huge accomplishment. At the completion of my current book, "Let It Boil over Twice," it has been over seven years since the brain injury. My brain has never and will never be fully recovered but I am doing great. There are some changes that will last my lifetime. Forward I go!

I will explain a little about how my brain injury feels; the person I used to be died on the operating table that eventful day in March of 2015. My family and I have adjusted to this new normal as best we can. It has been similar to witnessing the breaking of a mirror and then trying to put it back together. There is one piece that cannot be placed exactly as it was before. The Journey for Louise and I have sometimes been difficult. We are still a couple that have adjusted well to our many life changes and my new normal. I have a wonderful relationship with Louise and my two children. I have never been able to really connect with Louise's two daughters, maybe because they both live and work many miles away from Halifax Nova Scotia where we live, one in Ottawa Canada and one in Africa

While in the hospital a couple of friends came to visit me once. Only my family were my support group and constant companions. When the friends came to visit the conversation was mostly about them and all the different health crises that have happened in their families. I noticed within about twenty minutes into a conversation most people will ensure the conversation turns to focus on themselves. That change may be more subconscious to avoid listening to the hurt. I know the people who care about me the most are my family. They have stood by me through my most difficult circumstances. My family is my rock. My family including Louise is the type of family any person recovering from a brain injury needs.

According to Brain Injury Nova Scotia statistics, the number of people living with a brain injury are about sixty five thousand (65,000) folks in the province of Nova Scotia Canada alone. According to Brain Injury Canada, In Canada about 1.5 million people live with a brain injury. The brain injury Canada statistic states there are 165,000 brain injuries sustained every year, one person suffers a brain injury every three minutes, four hundred fifty two people every day. Not all brain injuries are reported immediately. After suffering a brain injury and surviving, a person's life expectancy is 9 years shorter compared to the risk of dying from several other causes. When compared to people without a brain injury, forty percent of all brain injury victims reach a good recovery, and in many cases still retain some issues that last their lifetime. There is a Brain injury Canada that advocates for folks with brain injury and most provinces of Canada have active brain injury associations who advocate on behalf of brain injury victims.

The provincial brain injury groups, such as the brain injury association of Nova Scotia and Brain injury Canada does everything it can to promote awareness of this debilitating injury.

Using a quote from my first book, "Threading the Needles of Life, Quote from Wendy Renzulla

"Brain injury survivors are extraordinary people, surviving under the most terrible circumstances, and they are more extraordinary because of it.

www.ingramcontent.com/pod-product-compliance
Lightning Source LLC
LaVergne TN
LVHW011719060526
838200LV00051B/2952